UNBREAKABLE

"A Journey of Survival and Truth"

Kayla Namio

Unbreakable: a poetry collection
Written by Kayla Namio
Cover design by Kayla Namio
Interior layout by Kayla Namio
First edition

Published by Franklin Publishers
Printed in the United States of America

For permissions, inquiries, or additional copies, contact:
Franklin Publishers
www.franklinpublishers.com

Feel free to use the blank pages within the book to help you figure out your journey through grief (journaling, doodling, etc.)

Disclaimer

This book delves into sensitive and potentially triggering subjects related to trauma. It has been crafted with care and respect, but some readers may find certain passages distressing.

Reader Discretion is Advised

This book is not intended to replace professional medical or psychological advice, diagnosis, or treatment. It is meant solely for reflective purposes.

If you or someone you know is affected by trauma, please reach out to a qualified mental health professional or seek assistance from a trusted organization or helpline.

Dedication

To everyone who was told they were too much, too broken, too emotional- and kept living anyway.

And to anyone who has ever survived what should have destroyed them

Author's Note

This book originated as a personal act of survival.

It marked my initial step toward healing, as expressing these words aloud can be incredibly challenging.

I never intended to share my thoughts with anyone.

For a long time, I believed my story was too heavy—too dark, too complicated, too broken to belong anywhere in the world.

However, silence is its own kind of prison, and I've spent too long confined within those walls.

I believe that my first step to my healing is putting it down on paper.

These pages are the truth I carried alone for years. They serve as a testament that healing is not a straightforward journey, that survival does not always feel victorious, and that vulnerability is not a sign of weakness.

I am grateful to those who remained, who listened without judgment, and who created a safe space for me to express my truth- thank you for your patience and love.

To my therapist—thank you for being patient with me

while I figured out how to say it out loud; this is my "out loud" for now. Your guidance has given me the courage to share what I spent so long trying to hide.

To my dogs and my bearded dragon—your quiet, unconditional presence has saved me in ways I will never be able to explain. You are the reason I keep going.

And to anyone who finds themselves in these pages- know that I am not writing these words because I have it all figured out or because I am fully healed. I am writing them because some days, I need to remind myself of these very things.

These poems are not the end of my story; they are the moments when I felt steady enough to try to believe in something better.

If you are still in the middle of it, still learning how to keep breathing through it all, please know you are not alone.

Your story matters.
Your survival matters.
You are unbreakable.

Before You Begin

To anyone reading these pages— whether you are here because you have survived your own pain or because you love someone who has— I want you to know this:

These words are not instructions or a manual on how to heal,Or a checklist for how to love someone who has been hurt.

Mainly because I don't have anything like a manual or instructions, and no checklist to offer— I am also here trying to figure it out and have been for years.

These words are simply a record of what it feels like to keep living when the world has tried to silence you. They are the truth I never knew how to say out loud, and the hope I am still learning to believe.

If you are a survivor:
I hope these words help you understand that healing isn't linear.
That trust can take a lifetime to rebuild, and that sometimes the best thing you can do is simply stay.

Some of these pages are heavy.
Some may feel too familiar.
Some might help you feel seen for the very first time.

Wherever you find yourself in these words, please remember:

You are not too much.
You are not alone.
You are not broken beyond repair.

We are survivors, and we can absolutely heal in our own ways.

For the Ones Who
Love Us

These pages are helpful if you love someone who has been hurt. We all want to thank you for wanting to understand while so many turn away from.

The stories are heavy, even when the words press against your chest and make it so hard to breathe.

Please know that nothing you read here is an accusation.
Nothing is meant to make you feel like you must fix what was broken before you came, and nothing is meant to make you feel blamed or burdened.

Sometimes you may feel helpless watching someone you care about relive the past. Sometimes you will say the wrong thing without even realizing it. Sometimes you will reach for words and find only silence. Sometimes your love will not be enough to make it better.

And that is okay.

We don't expect you to save us. We don't need you to have all the answers. We just need you to believe us when we say it hurts, and to stay when it would be easier to look away, and even need you to understand everything perfectly.

We need something simpler and harder. Believe us when we say it hurts, stay when it would be easier to look away. Be our steady presence in that which has felt unsteady for too long. Healing is not a straight line or easy.

Healing is a messy journey, we will have days we go forward, other days back, we will hide, and other days we will reach out. We will be angry at things you can't see.

This doesn't mean you are failing us. It doesn't mean we don't love you.

There will be some mornings when we are laughing and present, and nights when we are distant, quiet, and angry at ghosts you want to understand but can't see. We will shut you out, but it's not because we don't love you; we are learning how to feel safe within ourselves and outside.

Your patience matters. Your presence matters. Your willingness to stay matters more than you will ever know.

You don't have to be our perfect lifeline or speak flawlessly to be our comfort while trying to fix us in order to love us.

We need you to show up, and just keep showing up. It will show your love is steady, and when it feels small, it's far from being small.

In this world, we are told we are too much, not enough, unworthy of softness – you are proof someone will stay.

Thank you for being here.
Thank you for trying.
Thank you for loving us exactly as we are.

It's more than enough.

"Childhood trauma can lead to an adulthood spent in survival mode, afraid to plant roots, to plan for the future, to trust, and to let joy in. It's a blessing to shift from surviving to thriving. It's not simple, but there is more than survival."

-Unknown

Table of Contents

Prologue

I didn't want to write this book; it began as a journal entry and that's when I had the thought that "surely I'm not the only one feeling any of this."

I was scared to write something to share with the world- scared to peel back the skin of my memories and show you the bruises underneath that I still carry.

But I needed to.

Because somewhere, someone is trying to convince themselves that what happened to them doesn't matter.

That their hurt isn't worth naming. That their survival isn't enough.

If you've ever felt like your story was too heavy to be held, too messy to be believed, too dark to be spoken— these words, these pages, are for you.

I don't have every answer.

I am still healing.

Still learning how to trust softness after so many years of expecting the worst.

But silence is its own kind of prison. And I've spent too long locked inside of it.

This is me standing in the destruction.

Breathing.
Writing.
Refusing to disappear.

But if nothing else,

I hope these pages remind you:

You are not alone.
You are never too much.
You are never unworthy.
You are unbreakable, too.
You are not a victim.
You are a survivor.

And you deserve to take up space.
Exactly as you are.

"To live in the body of a survivor is to never be able to leave the scene of the crime. I cannot ignore the fact that I live here."

-Blythe Baird

Too Much

I've been told I'm too much—
too emotional, too heavy, too loud in my sadness.

Too much grief in my eyes,
too many questions in my chest,
too many feelings,
too many nights with tears,
too many nightmares I couldn't end.

I learned to tuck my too-muchness into smaller spaces,
fold myself down like paper,
to swallow the words that burned my tongue and throat,
to smooth the edges of my story
so no one would flinch or feel uncomfortable
of my truth.

To smile so big, it would cover the wreckage and
broken pieces.
To pretend that surviving didn't leave me raw and
trembling.
To pretend that I knew how to love,
Even when love still felt like a language I didn't speak.
To arrange my face to be presentable.

But even when I shrink myself,
even when I'm quiet,

20

When I vanish behind the polite versions of me,
that's when the parts of me ache the loudest.
When my skin buzzes with everything unsaid.
They still say I'm too much.

Too sensitive.
Too intense.
Too honest.
Too intimidating.

So maybe I am.

Maybe too much just means all of me—
unsoftened, unhidden, unapologetic, unashamed.

Maybe too much is exactly what I'm meant to be,
To stop editing myself into a version they can swallow.

And I won't apologize anymore.
Not for the way I feel.
Not for the way I love.
Not for the way I refuse to pretend my heart isn't
always breaking open, my head telling me I'm not
enough.
I am too much and not enough and everything at
once.
I am a million contradictions and inconsistencies.
Wrapped in skin.

I am tenderness that cannot be confined,
grief that will not be suppressed.
Hope that refuses to die.

I am the sum of every wound and every hope.
I am the voice that still rises,
even when no one wants to hear it.
I am the storm they whisper about
When they think storms only happen far away.
I am too much for the ones who cannot hold the truth.

I am too much for the ones who cannot hear the truth.
I am too much for the ones who cannot believe in me.

Too much for those who only want the pretty parts.
Too much for those who believe love should be easy
and healing should be silent.

So, call me too much.
Call me a storm.
Call me unreasonable.
Call me heartless.

I will never be small again.
Not for you.
Not for them.
Not for a world that keeps trying to cut me down,
To size.

But understand—
this is who I am.
This is who survived,
Who refuses to disappear.

I will never be small again.
I am here, entire,
And I'm not shrinking.

Too Much Interlude

I wrote this because I'm tired of pretending.

Putting it on paper seems easier than saying it out loud; paper doesn't flinch, or pity, or turn its eyes away when the truth is too sharp.

I've spent years making myself smaller so others could stay comfortable. But shrinking never made the loneliness go away—the kind of loneliness where you're alone in your own story, even when you're surrounded by people who are smiling and pretending you belong in their lightness.

If you've ever swallowed your feelings just to keep someone close,

I see you.

You deserve to be all of yourself without apology, without pretending, and without wondering if you're enough. I know how it feels to wonder if you're too loud in your sadness, too honest about your pain, or too overstimulated with all the thoughts in your head. I know how it feels to see the moment someone decides your story is too much for them to carry.

But hear me loudly when I say:

You're not too much.
You're exactly enough.
The fullness of your feelings
is not something to hide.

Those feelings are proof that you are alive and that you have survived.

If no one has said this to you before, I will be the first:

You don't have to shrink yourself to be who others want you to be.

You don't have to soften your truth to be worthy of love.

You don't have to edit yourself into a version that makes others more comfortable.

You don't owe anyone an apology for being real.

You are allowed to take up space. They should feel honored you shared your scars.

Please know, if you've been told you were too intense, too emotional, or too complicated—that was never about you.

It was about their inability to hold something honest. People who are afraid of their own darkness will call yours excessive. They haven't faced their own pain, so they want you to be quieter about yours.

Don't let them make you feel small, shame you out of your truth, or convince you that your softness is weakness. This world needs your too-muchness: Your tenderness, your grief, your wild hope.

The world needs the parts of you that refuse to be contained.

If you have ever felt like you're too much for the world to hold, then maybe this world isn't big enough for you.

You're here to show it how.

"The world breaks everyone, and afterward, many are strong at the broken places."

-Ernest Hemingway

He Took My Childhood

I was small when he decided my body wasn't mine.
Small when I learned how silence tastes—
like iron on my tongue.
Like a brick on my chest.
Like shame pressed into my skin.

I was small when I decided I'd rather disappear
than be touched by hands that never asked permission.

Small enough to believe maybe
I had done something wrong.
Small enough to believe that staying
quiet would keep me safe.
Small enough to think if I didn't look
anyone in the eye,
they wouldn't see the ruin behind them.

I wish I could tell the little
girl with shaking knees
that she was not to blame—
that her "no" was enough,
even if no one listened.

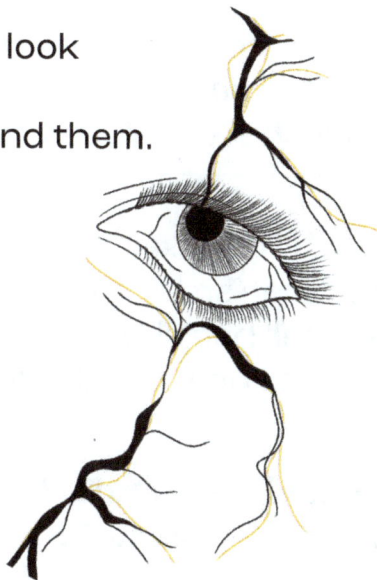

28

I wish I could wrap my arms
around her tiny body
and promise that one day,
she would grow into a woman
who could speak for both of us,
who could hold her own,
who would be heard.

I wish I could tell her that her worth was never measured
by the violence she survived,
that her softness was never an invitation,
that her silence was never consent.

I wish someone would have told her
that she didn't have to carry the secrets like a sickness,
that the shame was never hers to hold,
that surviving wasn't something to hide.

I wish I could tell her she didn't have to be brave—
that it was enough just to stay alive.
That she was already enough,
even when the world refused to protect her.

I wish I could sit beside her in the dark,
hold her small hand in mine,
and tell her she didn't deserve a single second of it.
And tell her that the nightmares don't have to be real.

That she was not ruined.
That she was not filthy.

That she was not unlovable.
That she was not broken.

That what he did was not love,
and that it wasn't her fault that no one stopped him.

I wish I could tell her that one day,
she would unlearn the lie that her body was a bur-
den.
That one day she would reclaim every inch of her-
self—
her voice, her skin, her boundaries, her worth.

I wish I could tell her that survival would not always
feel like shame—
that some days it will feel like power.

And that even on the days it still feels like drowning,
she is never alone.

He Took My Childhood Interlude

This is something I wish someone had told me:

What happened to you was not your fault.

Your body was never the problem.
Your softness was never an invitation.
Your silence was not consent.
Your stillness was not an agreement.
Your fear was not permission.

I know how it feels to carry the weight of someone else's choices on your back and to believe that maybe you could have stopped it if you had just been **louder, stronger, or braver.**

I know what it's like to spend years replaying every second, trying to find the exact moment it became your responsibility. You hunt for that one split second when it supposedly became your fault—as if it will reveal a secret you missed.

But it never was your responsibility to carry their choices.

You were loud enough. You were strong and brave enough.

Bravery doesn't always look like fighting back; sometimes, bravery is just surviving. When we are children, we are supposed to be protected. We should have grown up without learning the weight of someone else's violence.

You are not ruined, dirty, broken, or beyond repair.

You are a beautiful mosaic, a work of art pieced back together by your own hands. Each shard and seam is proof of your survival and courage.

The fact that you have survived at all is proof of your strength, even when you don't feel strong at all. The days you feel anything but strong, your survival is the proof. You are still breathing and trying to build a life— evidence of a strength greater than anyone should ever have been asked to carry.

Your body still remembers.
Your heart still tightens at the thought of it.
Neither of these make you weak.

**They just make you human.
They are the echoes of trauma**.

We are allowed to grieve what was stolen from us. We are allowed to feel angry, or to feel nothing at all. Emptiness is survival, too.

We can heal at our own pace. There are no deadlines, no comparisons, and no apologies required.

You should know you don't have to carry this alone anymore. The weight of what happened was never yours to carry.

No one deserves to carry it alone.

It Was Taken

I said no.
He didn't listen.

He took what he wanted,
and left me with the shame
like it belonged to me.

Afterward,
I tried to pretend I was okay,
that it wasn't what it was,
that if I stayed quiet,
maybe it would go away.

But it didn't.

But silence didn't erase it.

It followed me into every room,
every relationship where I smiled too quickly,
Every conversation,
every question I was too tired to answer.

And now when people ask
how I lost my virginity,
I want to say—
I didn't lose it.
It wasn't misplaced like keys on a table
It was taken.

Taken from a girl
who didn't know how to fight,
who didn't know how to scream louder,
who didn't know she was allowed
to call it what it was.

Taken in a moment
that rewrote how I saw myself,
that made me wonder
if my "no" would ever matter.

Years, I dressed it up in softer words.
I swallowed the language of violence
And replaced with words that made others
More comfortable.
I let them believe it was a mistake,
An accident,
Misstep of youth.

I am tired of pretending
it was anything else.

Tired of softening the story
so other people don't feel uncomfortable.

Tired of acting like it was some sad accident
instead of a choice he made.

It wasn't lost.
It was stolen.

Stolen by someone who decided my body
Was his for the taking.

Stolen in a way that scarred my trust,
Silenced my voice,
Made me believe,
I was nothing but the aftermath.

I am not the aftermath,
The silence,
The shame.

The shame doesn't belong to me.
Never did.
It belongs to him,
The one who took.

I will not carry his weight anymore.
I won't allowe my story to be rewritten,
To excuse him.
I will not allow my body to be remembered
As something lost.

And I am not the one
who should be ashamed.

It wasn't lost,
Or stolen.
I refuse to be the one
Who hangs her head.

It Was Taken Interlude

If you've ever swallowed the story so others wouldn't flinch—

if you've softened the language that burned like acid in your chest, called it a mistake, a misunderstanding, called it anything but what it was, just to make it easier to say—you're not alone.

You don't owe anyone a version of your story that makes them feel better about what happened to you. You don't need to hand it over in pieces just so they can feel safe, when it was what made you feel unsafe.

You don't have to use their words and call it "losing."

You don't have to pretend you consented or dress up your pain as if it were a fumble, a slip, a careless accident. Don't twist yourself into silence just so others can handle the sound of your truth.

You don't have to carry the shame he left behind. That burden was never yours. You are not defined by what someone took.

You are not dirty.
You are not ruined.
You are not unlovable.
You are worthy of tenderness and respect.

You are a whole human being, and nothing he did can strip that away from you.

If no one has ever said it plainly to you: it wasn't your fault. It was never your fault, not for a second, not in any version of the story.

Do not make excuses for the harm that someone else chose for you. You do not need to reframe your truth to protect other people from discomfort.

Your voice and your story belong to you.
Your survival is not something you ever have to apologize for.

You don't have to pretend it was anything else. Ever again.

The Aftermath of Silence

I swallowed the story whole,
Let it rot within me
Because every time I opened
My mouth,
The air turns thick
With suspicion.

"Are you sure?"
"Maybe you misunderstood."
"He didn't seem that way."

Their words pressed
my throat shut,
So I learned the art of silence-
A tongue bitten bloody,
A smile stitched over bruises.

Loneliness curled around me like,
I was choking,
But safer than the burn of their
Doubt.

I wanted to scream,
To set the room on fire
Just to prove the smoke
Was there.

Instead, I clenched my jaw,
Let the fury burn within my ribs,

Ember that refused to die.

Your disbelief was its own violence,
A slap I felt deeper than the first.

And I swore then-
If no one would carry my truth,
I would carve it into stone myself,
A monument of rage,
You cannot expunge.

For years,
I caged my voice,
Kept it hidden
Like a dangerous creature.

But silence only feeds the beast.
It grew teeth in the dark,
Claws in the heart,
It learned my heartbeat,
Waited for the right moment.

Now, when I open my mouth,
It does not whimper.
It roars.

My words slice through doubt
Like a blade forged in fire.
Every syllable
A wound stitched shut with truth.

You cannot dismantle me.
You cannot unhear me.

The Aftermath of Silence Interlude

Silence is not peace. It's heavy and sharp as glass—a cage within your chest.

When no one believes you, you learn to bite down on your truth until your mouth tastes of blood.

But silence is not safety, either. It is the echo of every wound, a reminder that your pain was never meant to stay hidden.

This is the place we begin:

In the quiet that almost broke us, in the hush that taught us how much a voice is worth.

The Men Who Didn't Stay

They loved the way I laughed
before they heard the way I cried.

They loved my body,
That curved under their hands
but never once asked what it had survived
To still be here.

They wanted the surface—
the good angles,
the bright eyes,
the soft skin,
the sex,
the "strong woman" story
with all the pain edited out.

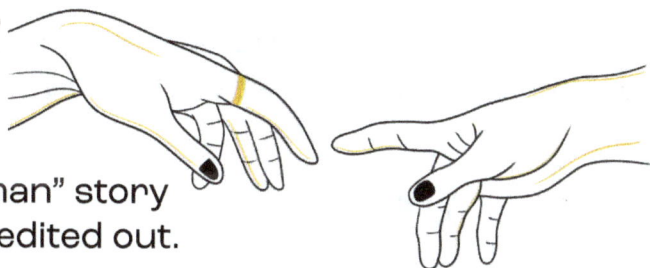

But I am not a highlight reel.
I am cracked bone and quiet survival.
I am a memory of screams they never stuck around
to hear.
I am a mosaic of the pieces that were broken into
shards.

They said they wanted real—
until I handed it to them.
Raw.

Shaking.
Human.

I told them about the abuse.
The trauma.
The diagnoses.
The days I couldn't get out of bed.
The nights I cried myself to sleep.
The nightmares.
The medications.
The fear.
The therapy.
The fight.

And they flinched.
Not because of what happened to me—
but because they didn't want to be inconvenienced
by it.

They kissed my scars
but never asked who put them there.
Held me like I was delicate—
then dropped me when I needed more than patience.

I was too loud when I spoke my pain.
Too quiet when I held it in.
Too much to carry.
Too damaged to love.

So, they left.
One by one.
Ghosts in my phone.

Unread apologies.
Half-healed heartbreaks.
Bodies that left no trace except
Heaviness in my chest.

And still...
some nights, I miss them.
Not because they were good,
but because I was lonely
and they were there.

I mourned them like deaths—
until I realized
they never loved me to begin with.

They loved who they thought I could be
if I were easier,
softer,
less... honest.

They loved my hope,
but not my darkness.
They loved my passion,
but not my grief.
They loved the version of me
that cost them nothing.

I used to think I was asking for too much.
Now I know I was simply asking for the truth—
and the truth was more than they could carry.

They called me resilient—
as long as I didn't need them.

They called me inspiring—
as long as my story was polished for their comfort.
They called me strong—
until my strength required their own.

I am too tired of being a museum for men
who only want to admire my ruins
without helping me rebuild.

I have learned that loneliness with my honesty
is softer than company built on pretending.

I forgive the girl I was—
the one who tried to trade pieces of herself
for love that was never real.

She did her best.
She wanted to be held.

But I am not her anymore.
I will not beg for crumbs of affection.
I will not dilute my truth to make someone stay.
I will not twist myself into a shape
That fits inside a man's fragile idea of
Love.

I was never made for men
who cannot handle women like me.

Women who do not pretend.
Women who do not flinch.
Women who will not apologize

for feeling everything.

I was made for truth.
For depth.
For fire.
For the kind of love
that does not run from the wreckage
But kneels beside me in it.

The next man will have to bleed beside me,
Unafraid of the weight.

or not come at all.

The Men Who Didn't Stay Interlude

I spent years believing love was something I had to earn by being easy, undemanding, and convenient. As if it was fragile, conditional, always one wrong step away from disappearing.

I thought if I was soft enough, quiet enough, and understanding enough, someone would finally stay. If I smoothed out every jagged edge, hid every scar, and made myself a comfortable place to land—then maybe I would finally be worthy enough for love.

But I've learned that love built on pretending is never love at all. It's a performance. It's survival. It's the slow erasure of everything honest inside of you.

Pretending doesn't build a home, just a stage. One day, you collapse behind the curtain, feeling empty, unseen, and unheard.

If you've ever made yourself smaller so someone wouldn't leave, I hope you know you don't have to do that anymore. Their leaving has never been proof of your worth.

You don't have to be less so someone else can feel comfortable. You don't have to hold your pain back to keep someone from flinching. You don't have to dilute your truth to fit with people who will never meet you where you are.

I wrote this for those who've been called too much, too intense, too sensitive, or too complicated. For those who have been left because they were honest about their scars, punished for their honesty, or abandoned because their grief was inconvenient.

You're not too much. You're simply more than they were ready to hold, deeper than they were brave enough to swim, and louder than they were willing to hear.

You don't have to apologize for it—not now, not ever.

You don't have to keep softening your edges, silencing your voice, or pretending your story is smaller than it is.

I don't flinch anymore when I speak the truth; I have flinched enough for a lifetime. I am done pretending my story is smaller than it is. I will not swallow my story anymore. I have swallowed enough silence to choke me.

I will not shrink anymore. I have folded myself into boxes that were never meant to hold me, and I have outgrown them all.

This is who I am: too much for the wrong people, exactly enough for myself, and more than enough for the love that will not ask me to pretend.

"What lies behind us and what lies before us are tiny matters compared to what lies within us."

- **Ralph W. Emerson**

They Look at Me Differently

When I tell my story,
Something shifts
people look at me differently—
like I'm fragile,
like I'm tragic,
like one wrong word
would split me in two,
like surviving makes me something
they can't quite understand.

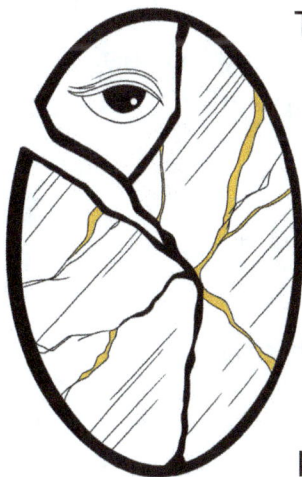

They tilt their heads with pity.
   They soften their voices.
   Their eyes fill with something be-
     tween,
   Curiosity and fear,
   Suddenly I am no longer,
   Me.

   They start measuring every word
   Like my ears are too delicate for
   Honesty.
   like I might shatter
if they say the wrong thing.

They say things like,
"You're so strong,"
but their eyes say,
"I don't know what to do with this."
Their eyes say,
"Please make this easier to hear."

They want the polished version—
the survivor's highlight reel.
Where pain turns neatly into wisdom.
They don't want the mess,
the ache that still lives in my bones,
the parts of me that never healed neatly.

They don't want the
Ending without the middle,
They want the beauty without the blood,
The miracle without the mess.

But the story doesn't go like that.
The story is ache that still lives within my bones.
The story is nights I still wake up gasping.
The story is scars that don't fade,
Memories that don't soften,
Healing that doesn't arrive on schedule.

And maybe that's why I stop talking—
why I pull the curtain back over my history,
why I smile and change the subject,
why I pretend I am simpler
than I really am.

Because being seen

isn't the same as being understood.
Because sometimes,
It's not the same as being understood.
It feels safer to be misunderstood
than to watch someone flinch
when I show them the truth.

I have learned that some
Want my resilience
Not my rage.

They want my survival
But not my scars.
They want my lessons
But not my loneliness

So, I quiet myself.
Tucking the story back inside.
I let them believe I am healed enough,
Whole enough,
Easy enough to sit across from without discomfort.

Inside, I'm still carrying it.
Inside, the story hums like a wound that never closes
Inside, the weight still presses against my ribs.

Truth is:
I am not fragile.
I am not tragic.
I am not a puzzle to be solved
Or a story to be neatly retold.

I am human.
I am messy.

I am both breaking and rebuilding,
Again and again.

And if that makes people flinch,
Let them.
I will not edit myself
Into a version that makes them comfortable
I will not polish my story
Until it shines so brightly
And they forget it was forged in darkness.

This is my truth.
This is my story.
It doesn't need to be easy to be real.

I am done pretending
That the truth must be softened
Just to be heard.

They Look at Me Differently Interlude

Have you shared your story and watched someone's eyes change—from curiosity to discomfort, from warmth to distance, from seeing you to studying you?

So have I.

I know how it feels to be held at arm's length the second you let someone see what you've survived. I know what it's like to regret the honesty, to wish you had swallowed the words back down, to wonder if silence would have been safer.

But your story is not too heavy. Your honesty isn't too much. Your past isn't something to apologize for.

Some people will never be able to hold what you've lived through. They will flinch, change the subject, and treat your truth as if it were contagious. That doesn't mean you should be silent. It just means you deserve people who won't look away. It doesn't mean you are unlovable; it's proof they were not ready to love someone real.

Your story deserves space. Your pain deserves to be

named. Your survival deserves to be honored.

You deserve to be seen and still loved. You deserve to be understood without having to edit yourself into something easier to accept. Your fullness deserves to be seen—not only the polished parts or the resilience, but the mess, the ache, and the days you still stumble. You deserve love that doesn't retreat when faced with the weight of your scars.

If you must choose, let them misunderstand you. Let them walk away if they cannot stay. But never abandon your own truth just to keep someone comfortable.

Your truth is yours and yours alone.

No one—not fear, not shame, not their discomfort—can take that away from you.

You are not too much.
You are not too heavy.
You are not unworthy.

You are proof of what it means to keep breathing after the unthinkable.

You are allowed to tell that story exactly as it is—without edits, apologies, or shame.

Adults Decided I Was the Bad Kid

They decided who I was
before I even knew how to be.

The teachers with tired eyes,
the babysitters who sighed
when I walked into the room,
the grown-ups who called me difficult
before they ever asked why I was angry.

I learned early that adults could be cruel
in small, ordinary ways—
the tone in their voice,
the roll of their eyes,
The way their faces closed
When I entered.
They didn't hit me,
Didn't scream.
the way they looked past me
like I was just another problem
to manage,
An inconvenience.

I was the kid who asked too many questions,
who talked too loudly,

who cried when things didn't make sense.
I was the kid who never fit neatly into a chair,
never learned how to be invisible.

The art teacher told me
I was awful at art—
that nothing I made was good enough
to hang on the wall.

So, I stopped drawing.
Stopped believing I had anything worth showing.

The PE teachers had it out for me,
year after year—
no matter how hard I tried,
no matter how small I made myself.
It didn't matter if I behaved.
I was already the bad kid in their eyes.
I was already the one given up on.

They called it discipline,
            but it felt like humiliation.
            They called it structure,
            but it felt like rejection.

            They never wondered
            what it cost me
            to keep showing up to places
            where I was already unwel-
            come.

            They never asked why I
            was so angry,

why I stopped trying,
why I looked away when they spoke.
They just decided.
They wrote the story of me
Without handing me the pen.
And I believed them.

I believed I was the problem
To be managed,
A warning sign,
A cautionary tale.

I carried their voices like echoes
Within my chest.
I bent myself into shapes
I thought they would like.
I practiced disappearing
So, I wouldn't take up so much space

But all the while
A small part of me stayed alive-
The part which wanted to draw,
To ask questions,
To speak loudly without shame.

They decided who I was
But now I'm deciding who I will be.

Their verdict wasn't the truth.
It was just the story they told
To make their lives easier.
I don't have to live inside,
Anymore.

Adults Decided I Was the Bad Kid Interlude

If you were labeled the "bad kid" before anyone bothered to learn your heart, I hope you know none of that was ever about you.

Maybe you were loud because no one listened. Maybe you were angry because no one protected you. Maybe you were restless because your body was carrying things no child should be carrying. Maybe you cried because no one taught you that your tears were allowed.

You were never too much, never impossible. You were never broken beyond repair. You were a child doing your very best in a world that decided who you were before you had a chance to become it.

I'm sorry the grown-ups failed you. I'm sorry no one saw the good in you. I'm sorry they saw only problems when what you needed was protection. I'm sorry they mistook your survival strategies for rebellion, your questions for defiance, and your feelings for weakness.

No one paused long enough to see the good that was always within you: the tenderness under the anger, the hope beneath the noise, and the brilliance hidden in places they refused to look.

You never deserved their dismissal, their harsh words, their rolled eyes, their impatience, or their cruelty in the name of "discipline." You deserved gentleness, patience, arms that held you, voices that reassured you, and teachers who saw your fire as a possibility, not a punishment.

Labels like "bad," "difficult," or "too much" can't take anything away from you. They were never truths. They were reflections of their limitations, their unwillingness to understand, and their inability to see you clearly.

You were never who they said you were.

You are more than the names they called you, the punishments they handed out, and the small boxes they tried to press you into. You are the proof that the "bad kid" was never bad at all—just a child wanting to be seen, loved, and given a chance to grow.

You deserve that love now, without condition, performance, or apology.

You were worthy of kindness.
You still are.

"I am not what happened to me, I am what I choose to become."

- **Carl Jung**

I Am Not a Burden

I am not a burden,
though sometimes
my mind insists I am.

I am not a weight others must drag behind them,
Not obligation disguised as a person.

I am not too heavy,
though my history tries to weigh me down
and make me believe
I take up more space
than anyone could ever love.

I am not unworthy of care
just because some days
I need more than I can give.

I am not selfish for needing rest,
Not broken for needing help,
Not unlovable for having limits.

I am not too much
for the right hearts.
I am not an inconvenience,
even when I am quiet,
even when I am tired,
even when I cannot hide
the ache in my chest.

I am human.

Worthy.
Trying.

I am the sum of every day
I chose to stay
when leaving would have been easier.

I am the sum of every time
I picked up the pieces of myself
and began again.

I am the small victories no one saw.
I am the nights I kept breathing.
I am the mornings I rose

When my body begged me not to.

I am allowed to take up space.
I am allowed to need help.
I am allowed to exist without apology.
I am allowed to be loved
without earning it,
Without shrinking myself to be chosen.

I am allowed to be held
On the days I am soft and on the days I am steel.
I am allowed to show my scars
Without explaining every one.

I am more than my survival
But my survival is also proof of my strength.
I am more than my pain,
But my pain is also evidence of my depth.

And all of this-
All of me-
Is enough.

Even when I doubt it,
When the voices are loud,
When the world tries to tell me
Otherwise.

I am not a burden
I am a life
I am still here.

That is enough.

I Am Not a Burden Interlude

If you are sitting in a room wondering if everyone would be better off without you, just know that thought is a lie. It's not the truth of you; it's only a trick of a tired mind.

You're not a burden.

You never were. Not as a child. Not now. Not in the quietest corners of your pain.

The fact that you feel deeply doesn't make you too much. It makes you alive. It makes you human. It makes you the type of person who notices beauty others miss.

The fact that you need support doesn't make you unworthy. It makes you connected and honest. It means you have not lost the courage to reach for someone, even when it scares you.

The fact that you carry old wounds doesn't make you impossible to love. It means you have survived what others could not imagine, and you are living proof of what it means to endure.

I know how heavy it can feel to ask for help, to need

reassurance, or to simply exist when your mind tells you you're taking up more than your share.

But your presence is not an imposition.
Your voice isn't an interruption.
Your needs are not an inconvenience.
Your existence is not a mistake.
You are allowed to take up space, to lean on the people who love you, and to be here—exactly as you are, without apology.

You are allowed to be tired, to cry, to heal slowly, and to ask for what you need—and still be worthy of love when you ask.

If you need to read it today:

You are wanted.
You matter.
You are enough.

Just by breathing.
Just by being here.

You are not a burden.
You are a heart still beating in a world that needs what only you carry, and that is more than enough.

Diagnosis Doesn't Mean Undeserving

There are days my brain feels like it's trying to break me.
Days when thoughts pile up like
Storm clouds,
Until the air within my skull feels
Electrifying.

Days my heart races for no reason,
my hands shake,
my breath won't settle.

Days I can't get out of bed,
can't answer the phone,
Not because I don't care
But I can't meet the demands.

Days can't remember who I was
before the darkness taking up
residence within me.

Days when the past comes back in flashes,
sharp as glass,
heavy as shame.

Days when a smell, a sound, a memory
Drops me back into a moment I never
Wanted to revisit.

68

Days when I smile so no one will ask,
when I laugh, so no one will look closer,
when I pretend, I am fine because it is easier than
explaining the ache.

Major Depressive Disorder.
CPTSD.
Anxiety so loud it echoes in my bones.
ADHD that unravels every focus I try to stitch together.

These are labels, not definitions.
These are explanations, not excuses.
These are pieces of me—
not the whole story.

I have spent years learning the difference
between who I am
and what I carry.

Some days, my mind feels like a battlefield—
chemicals and memories colliding
until I can't tell
where the pain ends
and I begin.

Some days, I am tired of fighting.
Tired of trying to prove to the world
that I am still worth loving
even when I am not easy to hold.

Tired of performing resilience,
So, no one sees how much it costs me.

But even on those days-
I am still worthy of love.
Still deserving of softness.

Still enough.

I am not my symptoms.
I am not the worst thing that has ever happened to me.
I am not broken beyond repair.

I am the girl who wakes up anyway,
who takes her medication,
who shows up to therapy,
who keeps trying.
Despite the feeling of
Climbing uphill,
Suffocating,
Needing oxygen.

I am the girl who still laughs,
even when it hurts.
I am the girl who still hopes,
even when it feels foolish.

I am the girl who still believes in something better.
I am the girl who refuses to apologize
for surviving,
Needing help,
Having a story that isn't tidy.

So, call me what you will—
diagnosed, disordered, difficult.

I will still call myself worthy.
I will still call myself human.
I will still call myself
enough.

Because everyday I stay,
Every day I reach for another morning,

70

Every day I keep breathing through the noise-
I am writing a story
Bigger than my pain

And that story is me.

Diagnosis Doesn't Mean Undeserving Interlude

If you have forced a smile so no one would see how much you were hurting, you're not alone.

I know what it feels like to be the one who seems okay on the outside—the one who keeps showing up, keeps performing normal, and keeps pretending the weight isn't unbearable.

The one who laughs at the right times so no one will notice the tremor in their voice and asks others how they're doing so no one thinks to ask back.

I know how heavy it is to carry a mind that turns against you. How exhausting it is to hide the shaking in your hands, the chaos in your thoughts, the sadness you can't explain. How lonely it feels to be surrounded by people and still believe no one can see you.

You don't have to keep proving that you're fine or smile just to make everyone else comfortable. You don't have to disguise your pain as politeness. You don't have to pretend you're invincible to be worthy of love.

You are allowed to be honest about the days that feel impossible. You are allowed to say "this hurts," to let your mask slip, and to ask for help without shame.

Your struggle doesn't make you less deserving.
Your diagnoses do not make you unlovable.
Your survival doesn't require an apology.

If you need to read this today, read it as many times as you need. Memorize it like a prayer and let it sink in:

**You're not alone in your darkness.
You're not the only one who has felt this tired.
You are not weak for feeling it.
You are not broken beyond repair.
You're still worthy of every good thing, even when all you can do is keep breathing.**

When all you can do is breathe, you are already doing enough. Even when you can't smile, you are enough.

And you don't have to hide that truth anymore.

Mental Health and Trauma

Sometimes I don't know where the trauma ends
and the diagnoses begin.

Is it the chemicals in my brain,
or the memories lodged behind my ribs?
Is it my wiring,
or the aftermath of surviving things
no one should have to survive?

The panic doesn't ask for explanations.
The flashbacks don't care about definitions.
They arrive unannounced,
Bypassing logic,
Reminding me the body keeps score
Whether or not I want to read it.

Trauma carved pathways in my mind—
deep ruts where fear still travels
without invitation.

Mental illness grew in the places
where I was never safe.
It rooted itself in the cracks
left behind by all the times
I wasn't believed.

All the times my voice trembled
And went unheard.

Some days, I hate the pills,
the labels,
the sterile names for all my hurting.

Some days, I resent the way people
talk about recovery
like it's as simple
as choosing to feel better,
Like it's a ladder I'm refusing to climb
Instead of a cliff I've been clinging
To for years.

Some days, I wish I could peel the diagnoses
off my skin
Like old stickers
and be someone new—
someone lighter,
someone easier to love,
Someone whose scars don't
Interrupt every single
conversation.

But I am learning to hold all the pieces—
the biology,
the trauma,
the survival—
without shame.

Learning that none of these pieces cancel the others.
Learning that even the messy parts
Are evidence of how fiercely I have tried to stay alive.
Because even if the pain never fully leaves,
I am still here.

Still showing up,
Taking the next breath,
The next pill,
Next step toward whatever
This healing should look like.

I am still trying.
I am still building a life in the shadow of
Everything.
That tried to
Take it from me.

Most of all,
I am still worthy.

Worthy of care.
Worthy of patience.
Worthy of love,
That doesn't require me to be
Lighter,
Easier,
Healed before it arrives.

I am not only what I've survived.
I am not only what my brain does on its hardest days.
I am not only a list of symptoms.

I am a person.
Alive.
Complex.
Still here.

And that-
By itself-
Is extraordinary.

Mental Health and Trauma Interlude

Your pain is real enough, valid enough, serious enough— I hope you read this and take it in.

You don't have to prove anything to anyone or perform your symptoms so people will finally believe you. You don't have to make your suffering look dramatic or photogenic to justify it.

Your trauma is real, whether or not someone else validates it. Your diagnoses are real, whether or not someone else understands them. Your body knows what it has been through, your nervous system carries the record, and your brain remembers even when your mouth cannot.

You don't have to apologize for the way your brain holds onto old wounds, your body flinches at ghosts or justify why some days are harder than others. You are in no need to justify why some days feel impossible, the simplest tasks feel like the steepest mountains, and not always able to "just get over it."

Healing doesn't look the same for everyone. Sometimes

it's slow, messy, means taking medication, canceling plans, or falling apart in the middle of a Thursday afternoon, or even in the aisle of a grocery store with a cart partly full.

It doesn't make you weak, dramatic, unworthy or broken. It only makes you human.

You are not too broken or too complicated. You are not a burden because you're still in process. You are not less because you're still learning to live with what happened.

You are simply someone who has survived- survival may be quiet and unremarkable from the outside, which is its own form of strength.

Your pain doesn't disqualify you from good things, your story doesn't make you unworthy of belonging, your humanity is intact, and your worth has not expired.

You do not have to earn compassion by proving you have wounds, shrink for needing support or apologize for it.

You are worthy of help, care, and love— exactly as you are.

"You are not your trauma. You are not your pain."

- **Unknown.**

Medication Mornings

Little pills lined up in my palm—
Tiny ovals, tiny circles,
proof I am trying.
Proof I am not giving up,
Even on the days I whisper that I want to.

They sit there like small witnesses
To all that I have survived.
Tiny shapes I swallow
like confessions,
like promises to keep breathing
Despite breathing feeling like punishment.

Some days, they feel like defeat,
a reminder that my brain needs help
just to be okay,
Be a version I can live with.

Other days, they feel like hope,
like maybe I can build a life
that doesn't revolve around surviving.

A life with mornings without panic,
Afternoons without collapsing,
Nights that no longer are battles.

Mostly, they are just another way I stay here,
another way I keep choosing myself
even when it's hard,

80

Even when the world, whispers
That "trying" should look like something else.

People tell me I don't need them,
that they're just pills to make the doctors rich,
that if I tried harder,
thought happier,
prayed more,
woke up earlier,
meditated longer,
smiled wider-
I'd be fine without them.

But they don't know
what I was like before—
how my anger was a wildfire I couldn't contain,
how I snapped at the people who loved me,
Burned everything near me
Even when I didn't mean to.

How the smallest things sent me spiraling.
How my hands shook from rage and panic,
How my heart raced itself raw.

They don't know how many nights
I lay awake,
asking why everyone was leaving,
never understanding
that my mind
was breaking itself apart
slowly.

They don't know that taking these pills
Isn't about weakness.

It's not about
Survival,
Courage,
Willingness
To do whatever it takes to heal,
Even when healing feels impossible

I have learned that taking them
does not mean I am weak.
It means I am willing to do whatever it takes
to heal.

I have learned to bless these small reminders
that I am still here,
still fighting,
still deserving of softness.

It's not loud,
It's quiet,
And unglamorous.

Medication doesn't erase who I am.
It makes it possible for me to meet myself
with more kindness.

Softening the edges of panic and despair
Long enough to remember
There is still a person here
Worth saving.

And if all I do today
is take my pills
and keep breathing,

that is enough.
It has always been enough.

Staying here is not failure,
It's proof.
Proof I am still,
Fighting,
Deserving of softness,
And I am still alive.

Medication Mornings Interlude

When you've felt ashamed of needing medication to stay steady, just pause here and let this sink into your bones: there is nothing weak about choosing help, nothing broken about needing support, and nothing shameful about doing what it takes to survive.

People will tell you otherwise. That you don't need it, that you're just making the doctors rich, that it's all in your head, that you'd be fine if you just tried harder, thought more positively, or prayed more faithfully.

But they don't know what it costs to keep breathing without it. They don't know how sharp the edges can get or how easily everything unravels when your mind is left untreated. They don't know how heavy it feels to live inside a body that keeps sounding alarms you can't turn off, or the panic that sits in your chest like fire, or the way depression pulls you under like an undertow.

They don't know how it feels to watch people walk away because your pain spilled out in ways you couldn't control, or to stare at the ceiling every single night, asking yourself why you can't be "normal" and wondering if anyone will ever stay.

You are not less worthy because your brain requires a little extra care. You're not less strong because of the medication that helps you stay. You are not defective for needing what others do not.

Some of us were handed heavier loads to carry. We were given bodies and minds that need more tending. That doesn't make you defective;

it just makes you human.

You're allowed to take your pills without explaining yourself to anyone. You're allowed to honor your healing without apology. You're allowed to be proud of the way you keep showing up for your own life.

Medication is not defeat. It's commitment and survival. It does not diminish your strength—**it proves it.**

It testifies to your courage to admit you need help and your strength to keep showing up for yourself in the smallest, quietest, most ordinary of ways.

It takes resilience to keep swallowing those pills every single day, not as an escape but as a declaration:

I am still here.
I am still trying.
I am still worthy of life.
I am not giving up on myself.

So, take them without shame. Bless the steadiness they bring and the fact that you are here to take them at all.

Medication doesn't erase your strength; it amplifies it. It doesn't make you less; it only proves you are more: committed, resilient, alive.

This is something to carry with pride.

The Night of Noise

The world sleeps,
But my body doesn't,
The voices in my head,
Doesn't.

It remembers too much.

The dark presses in,
And suddenly I hear everything-
Doors that never scraped,
Footsteps that aren't there,
The echo of voices
I wish I could forget.

Trauma doesn't whisper.
It screams in the stillness.
It turns every shadow
Into a warning,
Every heartbeat into an alarm.

I pull the covers higher,
As if cotton can muffle memories,
As if sleep will come
If I just lie still enough.

But the night is not silent.
It is full of ghosts,
And they all know my name,
My secrets,
The trauma.

So I take the medicine-
Tiny anchors,
To weigh down the noise,
To hush the noise,
So I can finally drift.

Sleep doesn't come naturally.
It has to be prescribed.

The Night of Noise Interlude

If you've ever dreaded the sun going down, knowing the silence will only make the memories louder, you are not alone.

When the world gets quiet, a body that has survived trauma can feel like it's screaming. Every creak of the house, every shadow, can feel like a threat . It's not your fault that your nervous system is still on high alert; it's a sign that you have fought to survive.

You are not broken for needing help to rest. You are not weak for needing medicine to find the peace that others find so easily. You deserve sleep that isn't a battle. You deserve a night that feels like a refuge, not a warzone. You deserve rest.

Hands

Some hands heal.
Hands that reach out without taking.
Hands that hold without bruising.
Hands that steady when you're shaking.
Hands that remind you softness is still possible.

Hands that lift you up, not to own you,
But to remind you of your own strength.
Hands that carry gentleness in every
fingertip,
Proving that touch does not have to be
pain.

Some hands harm.
Hands that grab without asking.
Hands that punish.
Hands that silence
Hands that teach you to flinch.
Hands that make safety feel foreign,
Love feels conditional,
Touch feels like something to endure
instead of enjoy.

Some hands say they're sorry
and never mean it—
the same hands that hurt you,
promising they won't again.

I have learned to tell the difference.

90

To feel the weight in a touch
And know when it carries a warning..
To hear the truth in a voice.
To trust the instinct that says—
this is not safety.

I have learned that I don't have to accept
every hand that reaches for me.
That I am allowed to step back.
That I am allowed to say no.

I will never again let hands touch me
if they do not know
how to hold me gently.

I will never again confuse control for care,
Or apologies for change,
Or pain for love.

Because I know now-
My body deserves tenderness.
My spirit deserves rest.
My life deserves to be held carefully,
By hands that do not take,
Or bruise.

My body deserves hands that,
Understand that touch is a language,
And mine only belongs
To those who can speak it softly.

Hands Interlude

When you feel ashamed for being cautious, needing space, or protecting yourself—you never have to apologize.

You're not too guarded, too difficult, or wrong for wanting to feel safe.

You have every right to decide who is allowed close and to listen to the knowing within your bones when something feels just slightly off. You can turn away from what unsettles your spirit, even if others don't see it or try to convince you you're imagining it.

Your body is not a place for anyone else's comfort. It's not a stage for others' desire or a container for someone else's control.

Your boundaries are not too much. They are not walls keeping love out; they are doors protecting your peace.

Your standards are not unreasonable. They are the bare minimum of what you deserve: care, respect, gentleness, and safety.

You are allowed to expect and demand gentleness. You are allowed to say, "This is how I will be treated, and nothing less will do." You are allowed to wait for hands that heal more than they hurt, for voices that soothe instead of silence, and for people who will honor your trust instead of testing it.

Take all the time you need. Move slowly, with wisdom, and honor the truth that you are worthy of love that doesn't bruise you, belittle you, or make you question your own instincts.

You're worthy of love that proves itself safe and trust that is earned, not demanded.

Until then, do not shrink your caution to fit someone else's comfort or soften your standards to keep someone near.

Your safety is sacred. Your life is sacred. And your "no" is sacred. You never have to apologize for honoring any of it.

"There are wounds that never show on the body that are deeper and more hurtful than anything that bleeds."

-Laurell K. Hamilton

The Girl I Was

She was small.
She was scared.
She was louder in her heart
than in her voice,
carrying entire storms
within her chest.
Letting out only
The softest whispers.

She was always waiting-
for someone to tell her
she was enough.

For someone to notice
the way her eyes begged
for safety.

Waiting for someone to see her,
Truly see her,
Not only the surface that
Was being held together

She was always hoping-
someone would see past her anger,
That wasn't anger at all,
Fear dressed in sharper clothes

Someone would understand
her restlessness,

that came from too much
weight too young.

Hoping someone would give her
A word she didn't know
For the sadness she didn't
Know how to name.

Deserving-
Softness rarely found,
Comfort without conditions,
Reminded existing
Exactly as she was,
Was already enough.

I wish I could hold her now—
tell her she didn't deserve any of it.

Tell her she wasn't wrong
For feeling so much.

Tell her the heaviness she carried
Was never proof she was broken.

I wish I could whisper to her
that someday,
she would learn to speak her truth
without shaking,
without apology,
without shrinking to make others
comfortable.

Tell her that someday,
she would grow into someone
who could protect herself.
That the little girl who felt

So fragile,
Easily dismissed,
Would one day stand taller
Than her own fear.

Tell her that she was never broken,
just unfinished.
A story still being written.
A song still finding its melody.
Surviving shall not be
Something to be ashamed of.

Survival is proof of her strength,
Even on days she felt it meant nothing.

And that even in her smallest,
most frightened moments,
she was already becoming
the woman I am proud to be.

That every tear,
Every silence,
Every trembling step
Shaping her into someone
Who could look back with love,
With compassion,
With reverence for the girl
Who kept going when
No one told her she could.

She was not broken.
She was not too much.
She was not unworthy.
She was becoming-
And she is the reason I am here.

Dear Little Me,

You were small and scared.

You were louder in your heart than you ever were in your voice.

You kept so much inside- storms that no one else could see- because you were afraid that if you let them out, no one would listen, or worse, they would use them against you.

I see how scary it was.

I see how you were always waiting-

- For someone to understand you.
- For someone to hold you without demanding you to be smaller, quieter, easier.

You deserved that, and you deserved softness, protection kindness and someone to look into your eyes and say, "You don't have to earn love."

I wish I could go back and hold you now. I would sit with you in the dark nights when you thought you were too much and hold you. I'd whisper the words you needed most:

"It was never your fault, and you were never broken or unworthy."

I would tell you:

"One day, you will grow into someone who can pro- tect herself, find your voice, and though it may still shake you will use it anyway. You'll learn that surviv- ing is not something to be ashamed of- it is something to honor."

You have never been broken then or now, little one. You were unfinished, just a story being written with a song that still is finding it's own melody.

In the smallest, most frightening moments, you were already becoming- becoming the woman I am proud to be now, and the one who can finally say to you:

"You were never too much, unworthy or to blame. You were always- always- enough.

I carry you with me still. I honor you and I love you. I will never let you be forgotten.

With all my love,

ME.

The Girl I Was Interlude

You'll always carry the little version of you inside your heart. Just know, you deserved better.

You deserved softness, protection, and gentleness.

You deserved someone to notice the way your hands shook, to tell you that you didn't have to earn love by being quiet, by being small, by disappearing so others could shine.

You deserved to be held without conditions, listened to without judgment, and loved without having to prove you were worthy first.

You deserved to be believed when you said you were scared. You deserved someone to look into your eyes and see the truth trembling within.

You deserved to be comforted when the world was too loud, not have your tears called "dramatic" or your fears laughed at. You deserved to have your voice heard, not silenced because it made others uncomfortable. You deserved safety you didn't have to beg for and comfort you didn't have to chase.

Because you didn't always get those things, you're allowed to grieve for the small you. You are allowed to mourn for every time you were blamed for things you couldn't control, left alone with too much weight, and made to make sense of things no child should ever have to understand.

You are allowed to mourn the childhood you should have had, the safety you should have known, and the innocence you were forced to trade too soon.

Be proud of the young you—for every time you kept going when it would have been easier to give up, for the way you found tiny sparks of hope in places no one bothered to look, and for the secret strength you carried when no one told you it was strength at all. Be proud that somehow, you refused to let the darkness take all of you away.

You are allowed to feel the sadness and the gratitude, the ache and the pride, the mourning for what you lost and the awe for the way you endured.
You survived so you could stand here. You survived, so that child you were would never be forgotten.

You survived to prove that, even in the silence and loneliness, you were and always have been worthy of being remembered.

If you've never heard it:

You were never too much.

You were never unworthy.

You were never to blame.

And you were always, always enough.

Then.

Now.

Forever.

Smile for the Camera

There are photos of me smiling—
bright, effortless, whole.

Snapshots that make life
Look soft and easy.

Proof for everyone else
that I was okay.

Proof they can scroll past
Without worry.

Proof that I am
Manageable,
Presentable,
Fine.

But no one sees the minutes
after the shutter clicks,
when my face falls back into grief,
when my jaw unclenches
when the smile slides off my skin
like something borrowed,
something fragile to be held
for a few seconds at a time.

No one asks
how it feels to pretend happiness
so everyone else can stay comfortable.

102

No one asks
what it costs to hold the mask in place.
No one asks
What happens to all the sadness
That doesn't make it into
The frame.

So I smile for the camera.
I smile because it's expected.
I smile because it's easier
than telling the truth
Why my hands are shaking,
Why my eyes look glassy,
Why I feel like disappearing
Behind my own face.

And then I break in private.
I cry in bathrooms.
I dissolve in parking lots.
I unravel behind closed doors.

Smile for the camera.
Hide the wreckage.
Make it easier to look at me.
Give them the version
Easiest to hold.

But just because I'm smiling
doesn't mean I'm okay.
Just because I'm smiling
doesn't mean I'm not breaking.

A photograph is a single second,
Not a whole story,
The smile is a pose,

Not a diagnosis.

Moment of composure
Doesn't erase the hours
Of ache that came prior,
The ones that come after.

Pictures always look bright.
Light will always look soft.
Survival looks like a
Practiced smile,
A heart trying to remember
How to beat in front of others
Again.

One day,
The smile in the photo
Will match the one within.

Until then,
I'm allowed to be both things at once-
Smiling and hurting,
Posed and unraveling,
Visible and invisible-
And still worthy of care.

Smile for the Camera Interlude

You'll always carry the little version of you inside your heart. Just know, you deserved better.

You deserved softness, protection, and gentleness. You deserved someone to notice the way your hands shook, to tell you that you didn't have to earn love by being quiet, by being small, by disappearing so others could shine. You deserved to be held without conditions, listened to without judgment, and loved without having to prove you were worthy first. You deserved to be believed when you said you were scared. You deserved someone to look into your eyes and see the truth trembling within.

You deserved to be comforted when the world was too loud, not have your tears called "dramatic" or your fears laughed at. You deserved to have your voice heard, not silenced because it made others uncomfortable. You deserved safety you didn't have to beg for and comfort you didn't have to chase.

Because you didn't always get those things, you're allowed to grieve for the small you. You are allowed to mourn for every time you were blamed for things you couldn't control, left alone with too much weight, and made to make sense of things no child should ever have to understand. You are allowed to mourn the childhood you should have had, the safety you should have known, and the innocence you were forced to trade too soon.

Be proud of the young you—for every time you kept going when it would have been easier to give up, for the way you found tiny sparks of hope in places no one bothered to look, and for the secret strength you carried when no one told you it was strength at all. Be proud that somehow, you refused to let the darkness take all of you away.

You are allowed to feel the sadness and the gratitude, the ache and the pride, the mourning for what you lost and the awe for the way you endured.

You survived so you could stand here. You survived, so that child you were would never be forgotten. You survived to prove that, even in the silence and loneliness, you were and always have been worthy of being remembered.

If you've never heard it: You were never too much. You were never unworthy. You were never to blame.

And you were always, always enough. Then. Now. Forever.

No One Wants the Wreckage

People love a good survival story—
the phoenix rising,
the triumphant comeback,
the perfect before-and-after.

They love the part where I am smiling again,
where the scars look poetic,
where the darkness becomes an inspiring anecdote.
They can clap for and then forget.

But no one wants the middle chapters.
No one wants the messy grief,
Sleepless nights,
Panic in my chest in the
Midst of the night
the days I couldn't get up,
the nights I wondered if it was worth staying.

No one wants to hear
about the anger that didn't go away,
the loneliness that followed me into every room,
the shame that clung to my skin
like something I couldn't wash off.

No one wants the wreckage.
The parts where I was still bleeding,
still breaking,

still trying to convince myself
that surviving was worth the cost.

No one wants the stuttering
Half-steps,
Unglamorous therapy sessions,
Pills lined up on the counter,
Mornings where brushing my hair
Felt impossible.

No one wants to hear
How survival can feel
Like a question mark
Not a victory lap.

But the wreckage is real.
It's not a footnote
And it deserves to be seen.

It deserves to be spoken out loud,
without shame,
without apology
Without waiting until it's
Neatly resolved that
Someone can stomach.

Because the truth is—
I didn't rise from the ashes
In a blaze of light and feathers
I crawled out of them,
On my hands and knees
raw and unfinished.

Covered in soot and silence.
I didn't emerge with wings.
I emerged with trembling hands,

A heart that still doubts itself
I didn't glow
I shook with exhaustion.

That story is just as
Worthy to be told.
Crawling is as sacred
As flying is.

The in-between matters
As much as the ending.

Survival is not only
The moment you rise-
Every second you choose
Not to stop trying,
Every breath you take when
Breathing still hurts.

The world may only want
The after picture.

I will tell the whole story.
The middle included.
The parts that are still messy.
The wreckage is real.
As am I.

No One Wants the Wreckage Interlude

Have you ever felt like your story only had value once it was polished, tied up neatly with a bow, and repacked as something inspiring? As if only then is it acceptable to share?

Understand this: you don't have to make healing pretty.

You don't have to sand down the rough edges, hide the bloodstains, or rewrite the chapters that still ache. The middle chapters matter. The wreckage matters.

Those nights you thought you wouldn't survive? They matter. Those mornings you woke up hollow and still had to breathe? They matter.

They are not blemishes in your story; they are your truth. And your truth is not something to be hidden just because it doesn't fit someone else's idea of resilience.

You're not required to turn your suffering into a neat ending for someone else's comfort. You don't have to translate your scars into metaphors that make people clap and call you inspiring. Refuse to package your grief into something digestible, pleasant, or safe.

You are allowed to be messy, unfinished, complicated, contradictory, raw in your hurt, and still searching for hope. You are allowed to let people see you mid-chapter, when the pages are stained with tears, when the sentences don't yet make sense, when the story has no clear resolution.

You are allowed to be a work in progress, to be unfinished, and to let the mess be seen.

Survival itself is enough. The fact that you're still here, still breathing and showing up in a world that tried to silence you—that is already enough.

Healing doesn't need to be beautiful to be real, inspiring to be valid, or finished to matter.

You are not a story written for someone else's applause. You are a life being lived, a body still carrying the weight, and a heart still beating.

And that—all by itself—is everything.

The Best Friend Stepped Back

It was the age of twelve that I learned
loyalty was something people liked to hear about,
but rarely practiced.

Twelve when I learned
Promises are only as real
As the convenience.

The lesson didn't come from
A book,
Or a warning from an adult.

It came from the school hallways,
Whispers that followed me like
Shadows.
The way I was smiled at on
Friday,
Turn into a mob by Monday.

They made me their target—
spreading rumors I was too young to understand,
stories about me that made my cheeks burn,
Before I knew what they meant.
Telling me I was disgusting,
that everyone hated me,
They said my name like it was dirty.

I defended her—
the girl I called my best friend,
the one whose secrets I carried like fragile glass,
The one I protected even when she was wrong.
the one I thought would stand beside me.

When twenty of them came down the sidewalk,
their faces twisted with delight,
Their voices raised like a single cruel song.
I thought she would speak up.
I thought she would step forward and say,
"It's not true."
I thought she would say,
"It was my fight too."

But she didn't
she stepped back.
Didn't look me in the eye.
Didn't open her mouth.

And I stood there alone,
Twelve years old.
Surrounded by people who hated me
Defending myself against accusations
I didn't even understand,
Alone in a crowd that had decided
Who I was.

That day something in me cracked.
That day, I learned loyalty is a word
people use when it's easy,
but abandon when it's hard.
But rare when it costs
Someone anything.
I learned that trust

was a currency I could never afford.
"Best Friend" can be just another word.

After that day,
I stopped believing anyone would stay.
I stopped telling people the truth.
I stopped letting anyone too close.
I built walls before I knew
How to name them.

Because I knew—
the second it got uncomfortable,
the second I needed someone to be brave for me,
they would step back.

And I would be alone
all over again.

I've carried that moment for years-
The sidewalk, the crowd, the silence.
It became a blueprint
For how I saw people.

How I read every glance for signs of betrayal,
How I learned to stand alone
Even when my knees would shake.

As an adult,
There's a part of me that
Is still standing on the sidewalk
At twelve.

Learning for the first time,
Loyalty is not a word.
It's a choice.

People will choose themselves
Always before they ever choose
You.

What I couldn't see then-
What I am learning now-
Is that failure didn't
Make me unworthy.

It didn't make me unlovable.
It didn't make my trust foolish.
It only showed me who they were,
And what I deserve instead.

The Best Friend Stepped Back Interlude

Sometimes we learn young that for some people—even those we trusted the most and called our best friend—"loyalty" is just a word. The kind they say but never truly carry.

They will leave you standing alone, and you must know it's not your fault. It's not your fault they let silence fall where their voice should have been , or that they let you take the blows, watching you tremble under the weight while they kept their hands clean.

Some people only stay when it costs them nothing. They'll promise to stand beside you, but when a moment requires courage and loyalty costs something real, they will vanish.

This doesn't mean you were unworthy of loyalty, asking for too much, or that you were impossible to defend. It only means they weren't ready or willing to be the friend you deserved. It means their version of love was smaller than yours , and they never understood that loyalty is not a convenience. It's a commitment.

You've always deserved someone who wouldn't step back when it gets hard or inconvenient ; someone who wouldn't treat you as optional when you have given them everything.

One day, you'll find the kind of love and friendship that doesn't falter when storms rise, measure your worth by the weight you carry, or expect you to stand alone just because standing beside you requires effort. One day, you'll know what it feels like to lean on someone and not fall; to speak and not be silenced; to break and not be abandoned.

That day, when that person walks into your life, it will remind you that you were not too much, not undeserving , and that you were simply waiting for the kind of people who understand that loyalty is not just a word.

It's a choice, a vow, and a love that stays.

"The deeper you heal, the higher you raise the bar on who has access to you."

-Unknown

Loyalty

I learned about loyalty
before I even knew what the word meant.
It wasn't in storybooks or classroom lessons-
It was in the school hallways,
Slammed lockers and whispered alliances
In a way secrets traded hands
Like money you could never afford to lose.

It happened in the giggles behind cupped palms,
The way someone smiled at me on a Tuesday,
And laughed about me on Wednesday.
It happened in the sudden cold shoulders,
best friends becoming strangers before
the end of recess.

I learned quickly that trust was a gift
Some people only asked for
So they could drop it
Just to see how fast they would break it.

I learned how to read faces
for the first sign of betrayal,
To notice the shift in a small glance
The edge in the loud laugh,
The silence that screamed something changed.

I learned how to be steel,
how to swallow and pretend
I didn't care

When I was left out on purpose,
Hide that I cared more than anything.

I learned how to keep my secrets to myself,
locked within my heart
Behind my ribs.
To carry the weight of it all alone
Handing them over
Felt like handing someone weapon
I learned how to be polite but distant,
Friendly but never exposed,
Present but never vulnerable.

I learned how to stop
expecting anyone to stay.

And by the time I was old enough
to spell the word loyalty,
I already knew
I couldn't trust it.
Promises rot.
Friendship fractures over nothing.
People leave without warning,
And call it growing up.

What I didn't know then-
But have learned now-
Betrayal says more about their smallness
Than about my worth.
That I wasn't unlovable,
I was simply surrounded by others
Who didn't know how to stay.

My trust was never the problem.
It was a gift,

They were careless.

Within the child in me remembers,
The sting of exclusion,
Her chest burning with humiliation,
How she taught herself
That closeness was dangerous.

She is the reason I built my walls,
The reason I flinch at times
When someone calls me "friend."

She's also the reason
I am learning to demand better now.
Loyalty should not be a trick,
Rare or something earned through pain.

Should be steady,
Safe, and will not apologize
For wanting it that way.

Loyalty Interlude

We shouldn't have had to learn when we were young that loyalty was something people only offered when it was convenient—and that's not our fault.

You didn't deserve the way they turned on you, the way they made you question your worth, or the way they made you feel replaceable in spaces where you should have felt safe.

Some people are too small to hold real friendship. They will ask for your trust without ever planning to keep it safe. They'll take your openness, generosity, and loyalty as if it were something disposable.

That doesn't mean you were foolish to give it.

It means your heart was open, you wanted to believe in something good, and you loved in the way you wished to be loved. And that is not something you should be ashamed of.

You're allowed to expect and demand loyalty. You are allowed to be selective, to take your time letting people in, and to build your trust slowly until you know it will not be dropped carelessly.

You deserve friendships that don't vanish when it stops being easy. You deserve people who don't flinch at your grief, walk away when your voice trembles, or shrink when loyalty asks for effort.

You deserve friends who are steady, who hold your secrets without turning them into weapons, and who show up on the hard days as much as the good ones.

You deserve those who stay—not out of obligation, but because they see you as someone worth staying for.

Until you find them, do not apologize for protecting your heart, for saying no to the ones who only knew how to take, or for expecting the loyalty you were always worthy of.

Because the right people will not call it too much.

They will call it love.
They will call it friendship.
They will call it home.

Comparing Traumas

They love to measure pain—
to line it up like a contest,
to decide whose suffering deserves more space,
To rank heartbreak as if grief can be weighed on a scale.
As if trauma had a scoreboard.
As if survival points could be tallied.

They say things like:
"At least you survived."
"At least it wasn't worse."
"Some people have it harder."

But healing doesn't happen in comparison.
Healing doesn't bloom in the shadow of "at least."
It doesn't thrive when you're told to be grateful
For what didn't kill you.
Healing happens in honesty.

My story doesn't erase yours.
Your pain doesn't make mine smaller.
There is room here
for every scar,
Yours,
And mine.

There is room
for all the silent nights,
Every story that trembles in the telling,

and all the shaking mornings.

There is room for the grief
That hides in the small corners,
The wounds no one else saw,
The heartbreak that doesn't look "big enough" to name.

There is room
for every story
that still hurts to tell.

You don't have to pretend it doesn't ache
just because someone else decided
it was too small to matter.

You don't have to silence your story
Just because theirs was louder.
You don't have to compete to be believed.
You don't have to measure to be worthy of compassion.

Hurt is hurt.
Loss is loss
Survival is survival.
None of it needs to be compared to count.

You don't have to earn your right to heal.
You don't have to prove the size of your suffering
Before you are allowed to name it.

Your pain is not a footnote.
Your grief is not less
because someone else's was loud.

The quiet ache in your chest

Is as worthy of care
As the screams that shook the walls.

You are allowed to claim your story
without apology.
You are allowed to say
"this happened to me"
without adding,
"but it could have been worse."

You are allowed to grieve what was lost.
You are allowed to feel the weight of it.
You are allowed to heal at your own pace.

Your healing is yours alone.
And it matters.

Always, completely, endlessly.

Comparing Traumas Interlude

If you have ever felt guilty for hurting because someone said it "could have been worse," you're not alone. You have permission to grieve anyway.

We've all been taught, in one way or another, to rank pain on an invisible scale, to measure our wounds against someone else's, and to minimize what happened to us because someone else "had it harder".

We've been told to be grateful it wasn't worse, as if gratitude cancels grief, as if perspective makes the ache disappear.

Pain doesn't need to be the biggest to be real. Your story doesn't have to be the darkest to deserve compassion

This is not a contest or a competition. There is no prize for "worse trauma" or a medal for "deepest wound".

This is simply the truth:

What happened to you matters.
The way it changed you matters.
The way you carry it matters.

You don't have to measure your pain against someone else's to decide if it counts. You don't need to justify your sorrow, explain why it still lingers, or compare your scars to prove they are valid .

Healing doesn't happen through comparison or by silencing yourself because someone else's story sounds louder.

It doesn't come from telling yourself you don't deserve to feel it. It happens through honesty, through allowing yourself to feel what is true, through letting yourself grieve what was lost, and through acknowledging the ache—even if someone else thinks it's too small to mention. It's not small to you, and that is all that matters.

You are allowed to hurt, to heal, and to take up space in your own story without apology. You're allowed to let your voice shake and still believe it belongs in the room.

You are allowed to know, without question, that your pain is valid, your healing is worthy, and your voice belongs here.

And anyone who tells you otherwise is wrong.

Trauma Felt Like Life

I didn't know it was trauma.
I thought it was life.

I thought love was something that hurt.
I thought silence was normal.
I thought fear was just part of waking up every day.

I thought the ache in my chest
Was something everyone carried.
I thought the way I disappeared into myself
Was just how you survived.

I thought tiptoeing around anger
Was just how you kept a home intact.

I thought the way I disappeared into myself
Was simply what survival looked like.

I thought the nights spent crying alone
Were simply what love looked like.
Belonging cost obedience,
Affection cost silence,
To be loved, I must be small.

I thought being small,
being quiet,
was the price of belonging.
So, I kept choosing what felt familiar.
The men who didn't listen.
The people who only stayed when I was quiet.

The rooms where my voice was too loud.

Because no one ever told me
that peace was possible.
That love could be gentle.
That love could be steady.
That life didn't have to feel like a battlefield.

It took years to understand
that what I called normal
was just another name
for unhealed.

It took years to see
That my patterns were not preference-
They were echoes of old wounds
I kept mistaking for home.

Even now, part of me waits
for the other shoe to drop.
Part of me flinches
when kindness doesn't come with strings.
Part of me still wonders
What the cost will be for gentleness,
As if it must be paid back later in pain.

Healing is not just learning new things.
It is unlearning everything
that taught me pain was inevitable.
It is peeling away every lesson
That told me I had to earn love
By bleeding for it.
It is rewriting that part of me
That equates quiet with safety
And chaos with love.

It is believing, for the first time,

that softness doesn't mean danger—
Safety is not a trick,
but safety is something I deserve.
Without bracing for harm,
Loved without disappearing.

And sometimes,
I still forget.
Sometimes I still reach for the familiar hurt,
Because pain wears the mask of comfort
When comfort is all you've ever known.

At times, I still silence myself,
Still shrink,
Still retreat into the child who thought
Survival was the same thing as living.

But I remind myself:
I am allowed to want more.
I am allowed to want peace.
I am allowed to choose love
That doesn't punish me for needing it.
I am allowed to call this longing home.

What I once called normal
Was not truth.

I am learning-
Slowly, haltingly,
With every small act of trust-
Is that a different kind of life is possible.

One that doesn't feel like holding my breath.
One that doesn't require my silence.
One that lets me stay whole.

And I am allowed to live it.

Trauma Felt Like Life Interlude

If you grew up thinking survival was the same as living, you're not alone.

No one teaches us what safety feels like when all we've ever known is harm. No one explains how to rest when your body has only ever known hypervigilance. No one hands over a map to peace when chaos is the air you breathed .

If you find yourself choosing pain because it feels familiar, be gentle with that part of you. Be gentle with the part that believes chaos means comfort, that flinches when things get too quiet, and that leans into the storm because stillness feels unbearable.

You're not broken for expecting the worst. You're not unlovable because peace feels strange on your skin. You're not defective for mistaking turbulence for love.

You were taught that love was something that hurt— so of course it feels confusing when it doesn't. We were taught that affection came with sharp edges, that care had strings attached, and that tenderness could turn violent in a blink of an eye.

Of course it feels strange when someone stays gentle, and your body hesitates to trust it.

It's going to take time to unlearn survival and to believe

that you don't have to earn safety by being small, being silent, or disappearing parts of yourself just to keep the peace. It takes time to trust that tenderness won't flip into cruelty, that calm won't erupt into rage, and that love won't leave you questioning your worth.

You deserve more than survival, more than fear disguised as affection, and more than staying small just to stay safe. You deserve love that doesn't ask you to suffer for it, softness without conditions, rest without fear, and a life that doesn't feel like holding your breath.

When you find it, and step into love that feels steady, gentle, and safe—call it home. Not the type of home built from survival, but the type of home where your heart can finally exhale, your body can finally unclench—and your story can finally begin again.

You are allowed to want more.
You are allowed to have more.
You are allowed to demand more.
You are allowed to call it home.

"The paradox of trauma has both the power to destroy and the power to transform and resurrect."

-Peter A. Levine

Hyper Independent

All of this made me
the way I am.

Hyper independent,
because I learned too young
that needing people was dangerous.
That reaching out a hand
Meant it might be slapped away.
That asking for help
Was just another way to invite disappointment.

Overthinking every word,
every glance,
every silence,
because I've been blindsided enough times
to know trust has sharp edges.
I have lived through enough betrayals
To memorize the moment someone shifts-
The pause too long,
The smile too thin,
The silence too heavy.

My brain replays these small betrayals
Like warnings carved into stone.

Overstimulated by my own thoughts—
too many tabs open in my mind,
None of them finished,
None of them closable.

Too many memories I can't close,
Flashing without warning,
Reminders of things I wish I could forget.

I try to rest,
But even in silence,
My head is noisy.

I learned to do everything myself.
To carry my own weight,
As if no one else could.
To fix my own messes,

Even the ones I didn't make.
To never owe anyone anything,
Because owing means vulnerability,
If vulnerability was a currency
I couldn't afford to spend.

Because depending on people
has always felt like a risk
Too sharp, too costly
It feels like building a house
On shifting sand-
Sooner or later,
It all collapses.

I became a fortress.
The one who doesn't
Ask,
Lean,
Or swallow the ache
Pretending it's strength.

And sometimes,
Quietly, secretly

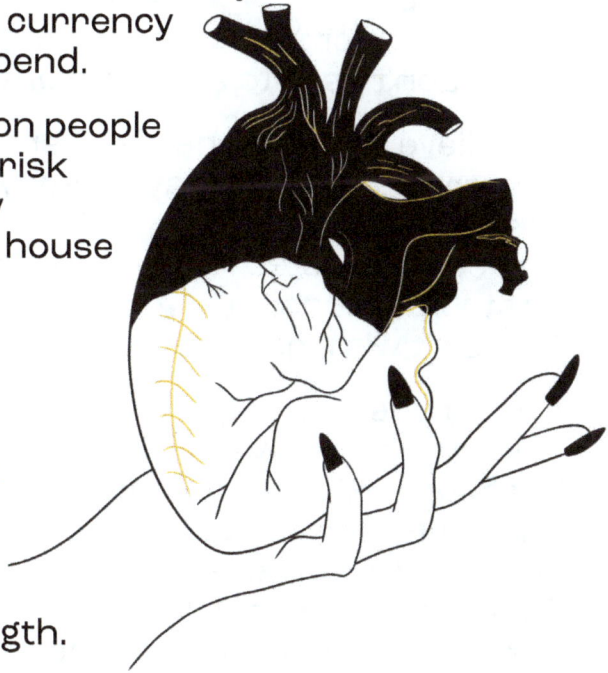

I wonder what it would feel like
to let someone help me,
to let someone stay,
To let someone in,
Hand over a piece of the weight,
And they see they don't drop it.

I wonder what it would feel like
To let someone help me
Without the fear of being indebted.
To let someone stay
Without rehearsing their leaving
In my head.

I wonder what it would feel like
To believe-
Just for a moment-
That I don't have to survive alone.

To believe that closeness doesn't always cut.
That trust doesn't always betray.
That sometimes,
Someone can step inside the fortress
Not to burn it down,
But to sit with me in its walls.

And maybe one day,
I'll let myself believe
That survival doesn't have to mean solitude.
That love can be steady.
That safety can be real.
That someone can hold me
Without me having to disappear first.

Hyper Independent Interlude

Have you been told you're distant because you learned to rely only on yourself?

You didn't become hyper-independent for no reason. You didn't just wake up one morning and decide that closeness wasn't for you. You became this way because your trust was broken too many times.

You learned the most difficult way that needing people could turn into punishment; the hands you reached for might be pushed away, that secrets you shared could be twisted into knives, and that love you gave so freely could be used as leverage.

So, you adapted. You survived.

Your walls were not built out of malice; they were built from necessity. You taught yourself to carry it all because you couldn't risk dropping it into hands that might let it shatter. This doesn't make you cold or difficult. It doesn't mean you're unloving or incapable of connection.

It makes you someone who has walked through loss and still found a way to keep going. It makes you resilient, even when you don't feel like it—because you keep showing up and moving forward with a weight that should have broken you .

You don't have to keep doing everything alone; being an island doesn't have to be forever.

You deserve to set that lifetime of weight down.

You deserve help that doesn't come with strings, softness you don't have to earn, rest without fearing what it will cost, and closeness that doesn't wound you.

It's okay to move slowly. It's okay to be cautious. It's okay if letting someone in still feels like standing on a cliff's edge. We don't heal from betrayal overnight.

When you are ready:
You are allowed to let someone in.
You are allowed to share the weight.
You are allowed to be held without breaking.
You are allowed to be cared for without owing anything in return.

No matter how long it takes, you are still worthy of that kind of love.

When you're ready, it's okay to let someone in.

"The paradox of trauma has both the power to destroy and the power to transform and resurrect."

-Peter A. Levine

Why I Go Silent

I go silent
because it's easier than explaining
the thousand thoughts tangled in my head-
Thoughts that move too fast,
Contradict themselves,
That never seem to fit neatly into words.

I go silent
Because I've learned the hard way
That honesty is not always safe.
That the wrong person will take my truth,
Twist it in their hands,
And hand it back to me as a weapon.

Instead, I swallow it,
Keep it locked away in my chest,
Where at least it's safe,
And can't be used against me.

I push people away
because I have been left before—
and I have learned,
it hurts less
if I'm the one who leaves first.

If I create the distance
Then the loss feels like a choice
Not abandonment.

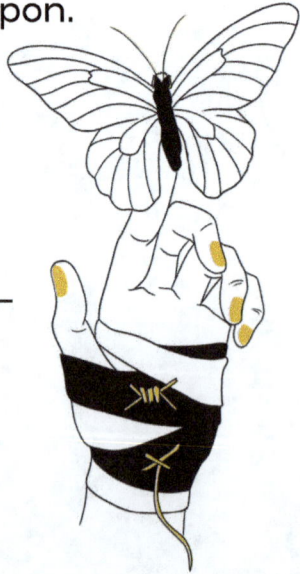

I shut down
because some days,
even the smallest conversation
feels like too much.

I don't want to socialize
because pretending to be okay
costs more than I can afford.
The mask feels heavier
Then the loneliness.

I am quiet
not because I don't care,
but because caring has made me tired.
Because I'm holding everyone else's stories
While mine sits unheard
It's drained me hollow

I am distant
not because you don't matter,
but because I don't know
how to be close
without feeling like I might break.

Intimacy feels like risk,
Like exposure,
A cliff, I don't know if I can survive the fall.

This is not rejection.
This is not indifference.
This is not proof that I don't value you.

This is survival.
This is my body remembering what hurt,
My heart choosing the quiet
Over the ache of being misunderstood.

This is the only language I know
When everything inside me is too loud.

Sometimes, silence is not absence-
It is protection.
It's the space I take,
To gather myself back together,
The distance I need
To keep breathing.

And sometimes,
it's the only way I know how to stay.

Why I Go Silent Interlude

Have you gone quiet and worried people would think you stopped caring? Understand this:

The silence doesn't mean you love any less or that you don't care. It doesn't mean you're cold or selfish.

Silence is sometimes what happens when you've carried too much for far too long, with few people noticing the weight you're carrying. It is the language of a heart that has been stretched thin and needs space to find safety again .

People won't always understand why you need distance, why you cancel plans, why you disappear into yourself, or why you choose the safety of your own company over the noise of a crowded room.

They might call it withdrawal, but they might not be aware that it is survival.

Your need for space doesn't make you unworthy of love. Your absence doesn't erase your presence. Your distance doesn't mean you've disappeared.

You don't owe the world a performance of happiness just to make others feel more comfortable. You don't have to smile when your chest is aching or explain every quiet day, every canceled plan, and every time you vanish for the sake of your own sanity .

You are allowed to rest, to pause, and to step back without apologizing for it.

The people who love you will still be here when you're ready to come back. They are the ones who see you—not just the shining version of yourself, but the real you. They will stand by you as you find your footing again .

Until then, let yourself breathe. Go quiet without shame, and remember your worth has never depended on how loud you are, how visible you are, or how easy you make it for others to understand you.

Even in your silence, you are still loved.
Even in your absence, you still matter.
Sometimes quiet is not disappearing; it's healing .
You are allowed to heal.

"Trauma catastrophically shatters our sense of connectedness to self."
-Judith Herman's Trauma Theory

Learning Love Again

I had to learn everything in reverse.
I had to untangle years of lies
Before I could even begin to understand the truth.

That love wasn't something that hurt.
That touch didn't have to feel like flinching.
That consent wasn't something you whispered
hoping it would be enough.

I spent years believing my body was just a thing
people took without asking.
A thing I owed to anyone who wanted it.
A thing I could never fully reclaim.

I believed disappearing was normal.
That closing my eyes,
Leaving my body behind during sex,
Was the only way to survive it.
I carried that numbness like armor.
Swallowing panic like medicine.
Wearing shame that never belonged to me,
But fit me like a second skin.

It took twenty years
to unlearn the vanishing act.
To stop confusing silence with safety,
to peel shame from my skin,
To unlearn the shame
that wasn't mine to begin with.

I didn't know
that it could feel good.
That it could feel safe,
Warm,
steady.

That it could feel like something I chose,
instead of something I survived.

I didn't know
that wanting was allowed.

That pleasure was a birth-
right,
not a confession.

I didn't know
that I could look someone
in the eye
and say "yes,"
and mean it.

It took twenty years
to understand
that my body is still mine.
That my "no" is final.
That my "yes" is sacred.

And for the first time,
I am learning
that I am allowed to enjoy this life—
even the parts I was taught

to fear.

I am allowed to live in this body
Without apology,
Fear,
Shame.

I can love this life-
The parts once feared,
Parts once believed were
Ruined.

None of it was ever ruined.
Not me.
Not this body.
Not my right to want.
Not my right to stay.

I am still here.
I am still mine.

Learning Love Again Interlude

If you have felt as if your body wasn't your own, or looked in the mirror and felt a stranger staring back, understand this: **it is still yours.**

It always has been. Even in the moments it felt stolen and the years it felt like a cage instead of a home. I know what it's like to carry the past into every moment of closeness—to wonder if you will ever be able to trust your own desire, your own voice, your own "yes," without hearing the echoes of someone else's choices.

I know how long it can take to believe that wanting is not shameful. That pleasure is not something to be earned by being healed enough, good enough, or worthy enough

That your body can be more than a reminder of what was taken; it can be a place you come home to instead of a place you abandon.

It is not your fault that it took time to unlearn what was done to you, or that trust feels like a foreign language, or that your chest tightens at the thought of intimacy. It's not your fault that safety feels foreign.

It can take years to learn that closeness can be tender,

intimacy can heal instead of wound, and desire can be holy instead of haunting.

You're allowed to take as long as you need—to say no without guilt, to say yes without fear, to learn the rhythm of your own body, to follow it into joy, and to let yourself stay present long enough to feel pleasure without apology

If no one has ever told you this: Your body is still yours. It wasn't ever ruined, and it is not broken beyond repair. This body belongs to you, and only you.

Your pleasure, desire, and softness still matter. You deserve a love that never asks you to disappear or rewrite your "no" into silence. You deserve a love that holds you gently and listens when you tremble. Love should wait for the moment you choose to open—celebrating that it was your choice to make and yours to give.

When you are ready, whether it be today, tomorrow, or years from now—something to remember:

You are allowed to take up space in your own skin. You are allowed to want and to stay. Your body is still yours, and you are still worthy of coming home to it.

The Ones Who Save Me

There are four dogs
and a bearded dragon
who don't know
they've saved my life
more times than I can count.

They don't know
that when the darkness gets heavy
and the air feels too thick to breathe,
I stay because I can't imagine
their faces waiting for me
and no one coming home.

They don't know
that every time I thought about leaving,
I thought about their faces-
their bowls, toys, and
the way each one leans into me
like I'm gravity.

They don't know that no one
could love them
in the way I do,
with all my faults,
with all my seams still showing.

Each one came into my life
when I was at my lowest,
was sure I didn't deserve-

anything good. They arrived like tiny miracles,
Unaware they were building a lifeline
just by existing.

Their names became anchors
when everything else felt untethered.
Their paws, their scales, their bright eyes
reminded me there was still something soft
and innocent,
and worth staying for
in this world.

I have learned the hard way
that I can't fill every hollow place
with something alive.

That I can't collect creatures
to heal what I haven't faced in myself.

But still—
they are the reason I get out of bed.
They are the reason I keep breathing.
They are the reason I stay.

And if all I ever did
was to be their person,
it would be enough.

Because they don't care about my trauma.
They don't care about my diagnoses.
They don't care how many times I've fallen apart.

They just care that I'm here.
They just care that I love them.

And sometimes,

that is what saves me.

If all I ever did
was to be their person,
if all I ever did
was make sure they were fed, safe,
and loved beyond question-
it would be enough.

Sometimes survival
isn't big speeches
or clean victories.

Sometimes it's the quiet promise
you make to a heartbeat smaller than yours:
I will be here.
I will come home.
I will keep going.

And sometimes,
that promise
is what saves you.

The Ones Who Save Me Interlude

Some of us stay for the ones with fur, scales, feathers, or even pattering little feet. They never asked you to be anything but exactly who you are.

Hold them close, like the lifelines they are, like the anchors that tether you here when everything else feels shaky.

This type of love is not small. It is not weakness. And it's not shameful to admit that their existence keeps you breathing. Sometimes the most honest reasons are the simplest:

The sound of paws on the floor when you walk through the door, the slow blink of trust from a cat curled in sunlight, the soft weight of a rabbit against your chest, or the laughter of your children—all of them believing you will always come back .

No human words can ever measure up to that. No applause, no compliment, no promise of "you're so strong". Because their love isn't a performance. It is survival woven into fur and feathers, into scales and soft noses, into the way they press their whole lives into your waiting hands.

You are not alone in this; there are so many hearts that stay beating because of the quiet responsibility of care and the silent agreement: "**You** keep me safe, and I'll keep you here".

Being their person is not small or an afterthought. It is enough. It is brave to choose them over the darkness, and holy to build your life around the ones that cannot speak your language—but know your soul. It's sacred to keep going because they depend on the rhythm of your breath to keep their world alive.

And if all you can do today is pour food into their bowl, open the cage, refill the water dish, or whisper their name—that is still everything. It is love, purpose, and survival.

If you ever doubt your worth, look into their eyes. See the way they light up at the sound of your footsteps and feel the way they lean against you like you are the safest place they know.

They don't care if you're broken, whole, if you stumble or fall, or anything else except exactly yourself.

They already know—you are home.

"Trauma catastrophically shatters our sense of connect-edness to self."

-Judith Herman's Trauma Theory

Softness Is Not Weakness

We've been made to feel ashamed for needing gentleness and having the craving of softness in a world that worships steel-

Wanting love is not weakness, safety is not failure, and tenderness is not something we shall apologize for.

You were not born hardened. That first cry you had was not a battle cry- it was a plea for comfort, arms to hold you, and someone to answer.

You learned to build walls because you had to in order to keep the danger out. You learned to be strong because the world gave you no choice.

But there is nothing small about softness.
There is nothing weak about wanting someone to hold you, to understand you, to stay when it's messy.

Somewhere along the way, you were taught that vulnerability was dangerous and a liability, letting anyone close, which would cost more than you could afford to lose. That letting someone in would cost you more than you could survive losing.

And maybe it did once. The hurt was real and sharp enough to make you swear that wall would never be taken down again.

Your heart survived all of it so far, and it still beats with a quiet truth.

We deserve gentleness, love that does not demand you to be perfect or unbroken to be worthy of it. You deserve the safety that does not expire when you fall apart.

Your softness is not a flaw to be hidden or a weakness. It is proof that no matter what tried to harden you, there is still something tender inside you worth protecting. The world did not succeed in hardening your softness; you still have something tender inside of you, still something worth alive and protecting.

You are allowed to want a life that feels safe.
You are allowed to ask for love that doesn't make you shrink.
You are allowed to be as soft as you need to be, and to breathe without bracing for impact.

And anyone who calls that weakness
has never understood true strength.
True strength is not a wall.

It is the hand that dares
to open the gate. It is the
heart that dares to risk
love again, even after being
broken. It is the courage to
stay soft despite the world
that is trying to turn you
into stone.

That softness is your power.

No one can take it from you.

Softness Is Not Weakness Interlude

If you've been taught that your gentleness is a liability, I want you to hear this: **your softness is a superpower.**

In a world that rewards hardness and confuses cruelty with strength, your ability to stay tender is an act of rebellion. They will mistake your empathy for weakness and your compassion for naivete, but you know the truth. It takes incredible strength to keep an open heart. It takes courage to choose gentleness when you've been met with harm.

Your softness is not a flaw; it is your proof that the world has not succeeded in breaking your spirit. You are allowed to be soft. You are allowed to crave gentleness. And you are not weak for wanting love that doesn't hurt.

You're So Strong

"You're so strong," they say—
as if it's an award to hang on the wall,
as if it's a compliment that should make me smile.

They say it like survival is a talent,
as if they're proud of me
for enduring what they themselves would never en-
dure,
without ever asking what it cost me to endure it.

They say it with soft eyes,
like they're looking at something powerful,
something admirable—
but their gaze never reaches the nights
I begged the walls to be quiet.

They don't see the mornings
I sat on the edge of my bed
and wondered if getting up was worth it.

They don't see-
the pills lined up on the nightstand,
the therapy where my voice cracked and broke,
the moments I tried to slip out of my own life quietly,
hoping no one would notice.

They don't see how tired I am
of holding the world up with my shaking hands.

They don't understand
that "strength" can be just another mask,
another costume I strap on each morning,
because saying "I'm not okay"
feels dangerous.

I don't want to be strong.
I want to be safe.
Soft.
Seen.

I want to be held
without having to prove I've earned it.
I want a place where my breath doesn't feel heavy,
where I can unravel
and not be punished for the threads.

But instead, I keep standing.
Keep smiling just for them.
Keep surviving for myself.
Laughing in the right places,
nod when they say how inspiring I am,
fold my pain neatly behind my back like a hidden scar.

They call it strength,
but I know better.
It isn't a victory banner.
It isn't a badge of honor.
It's the last thing left of me
after everything else has been burned away.

Strength, to me, is not glory.
It's the flicker of a candle in a room without windows.
It's the heartbeat that refuses to quit
even when you wish it would.

It's the quietest form of survival—
not triumphant, not clean,
but still, somehow, alive.

Surviving what they'd never survive.
And that is what I carry.

Not their version of strength,
but my own:

the fragile, relentless kind
that isn't pretty enough to frame
but still keeps me here.

You're So Strong Interlude

If you have been called strong, and it's never sounded like praise but like a reminder that there was no other choice—you are not alone .

Strength isn't always bravery, fire, or fight. Sometimes it's exhaustion, survival, and what's left when there is nothing else to be. Sometimes survival feels like crawling—the type that doesn't earn applause but still matters.

People say, "You're so strong," thinking it's a compliment, without realizing how heavy it lands . They don't realize it sounds a lot like, "You don't get to fall apart". They don't see that this compliment can feel like a cage.

You don't have to keep being strong for everyone else or pretend you're unbreakable. You don't have to keep holding it all together or wearing the mask of the unbreakable when inside you are aching to rest.

It is okay to admit you are tired, to let the tears flow, and to lay down the armor. You are allowed to want tenderness more than resilience. You are allowed to crave arms that hold you instead of words that command, to want silence instead of pep talks, and to be seen in your fragility instead of your endurance .

This isn't a performance.

You are not required to keep standing when your legs are shaking, or to smile when your heart is unraveling. In your humanness—in the breaking, the resting, the asking—you are still worthy and always have been.

You are allowed to be human, not just strong.

You are already enough, even when you're not holding it all together.

"The deeper you heal, the higher you raise the bar on who has access to you."

-Unknown

For the Days You Feel Like You're Failing

Today may feel too heavy to carry, if you are tired of trying, if your bones ache from holding up the weight of another sunrise, and wondering whether any of this work will ever be enough—

You are not failing.

Healing is not a straight line. It bends and folds.

It loops back on itself like a river carving stone.

Some days you will feel like you have moved backward, like you've lost every inch you fought for. Some days, you will question whether you have made any progress at all, or if any of this pain has even shifted at all.

That does not mean you are failing or broken beyond repair. It means you are still healing, your heart is still doing its work, quietly, invisibly, even on the days you can't feel it.

You are allowed to have days when you can't be brave.

You are allowed to have days when you don't get out of bed because it feels like you're climbing Mount Rushmore, so it's easier to stay in the safety of the

covers instead.
You are allowed to feel tired of fighting and letting the armor slide off your shoulders.

It doesn't make you weak. It makes you human.

You have survived every day that tried to break you. You have kept breathing through every night you thought you wouldn't. You have continued to show up in a world that did not always deserve your softness and has not always earned it.

That is enough, it's not small- It's a miracle. Even on the days you can't believe it, it is still enough, and the nights you can't believe it is still enough.

You don't have to prove your worth by always being okay.
You don't have to measure your progress against anyone else's timeline or their version of healing.

Your healing is yours. It will take as long as it takes - at the pace your body and soul and body require.

And you are still worthy of love exactly as you are— even if all you did today was survive.

That, too, is sacred work.

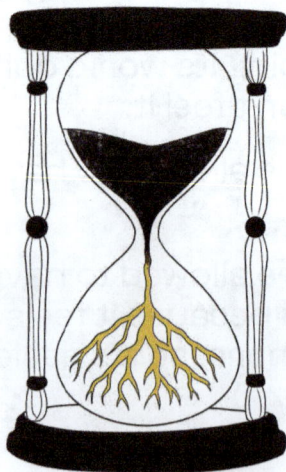

Survivor's Anthem

They thought I would
Disappear into the ruin
They left behind,
Like a ghost in a
Haunted house.

A whisper that's
Not heard.

A scar nobody
Could trace.

But ashes don't
Stay ashes.

Give them breath,
Give them time-
And they turn to soil,
To roots,
To life that refuses
To vacate.

I have been silence,
I have been fury,
I have been the echo,
No one wanted to hear.

Now I stand-
Not healed,
Not whole,

But **unbreakable.**

Every fracture is a map.
Every scar is proof.

And my voice-
Is the hymn
That outlived the hurricane.

Survivor's Anthem Interlude

This is not only my story; it belongs to anyone who has walked through this fire and come out scarred but still standing.

For the ones who doubted themselves, questioned their worth, and carried the shame that was never theirs to hold.

This is for you as well.

We may never erase the past, but we can sing louder than it.

Our voices, together, become the anthem they tried to silence.

Answer

No.
I am not trash.
I am not used up.
I am not ruined.

I am not the bruises.
I am not the silence.
I am not the nights
that nearly swallowed me whole.

My trauma is a chapter,
not the title of my life.
It carved scars, yes,
but scars are proof of healing,
not proof of damage.

I will not bow
to the lies it left in my head.
I am not waste.
I am not shame.
I am not yours anymore.

I am still mine.
And that—
that is everything.

Answer Interlude

Hear this, and let it sink into your bones: You are not what they did to you. You are not the names they called you. You are not the shame they left you with.

Your trauma is a part of your story, but it is not your identity. The scars are proof of healing, not proof that you are "damaged goods."

You are not ruined. You are not disposable. You are not trash.

You are a whole person, and you are still yours. That is, and always will be, everything.

When Freedom Is Another Cage

The bruises faded.
The shouting silent.
The door closed behind you—
nevertheless,
I was not free.

The silence was heavier
than your fists.
The emptiness louder
than your voice.

People said,
"You should be happy it's over."

But they didn't see
how loneliness curled itself
into my ribs,
how the quiet
kept me company
like a ghost I never summoned.

Survival is not the same as living.
Sometimes freedom feels
like another type of cage.

But slowly,
the silence softened.

It stopped sounding like you
and started sounding like me.

I made coffee without fear.
I laughed once,
and the sound startled me—
like a bird taking flight
within my chest.

Loneliness became space.
Space became breath.
Breath became the start
of something I thought I lost—

myself.

When Freedom Is Another Cage Interlude

If you've escaped, only to find that freedom feels empty and terrifying, your feelings are valid.

No one talks about this part—the deafening silence after the chaos, the loneliness that replaces the fear. People expect you to be happy, but you're grieving a life you knew, even if it was one that hurt you.

This is a normal part of healing. You are not ungrateful for feeling lost. You are simply unlearning a lifetime of survival. Be patient with yourself. That silence that feels so heavy? It will soften. That emptiness? It is not a cage; it is just space.

And you will learn, slowly, how to fill it with your own voice, your own choices, and your own peace.

The Touch

For a long time,
I treated touch like a weapon,
flinched from it,
hid from it,
feared what it could undo in me.

But slowly—
I began to rewrite it.

A hand grazing mine
did not have to mean danger.
A hug could be secure,
not suffocating.
My own fingertips on my skin
could mean comfort,
not survival.

I practiced in silence:
pressing lotion into my arms,
laying my palm over my heart,
reminding my body—
you are mine first.

And maybe one day,
I will let another person close,
not because I am forced,
but because I decide it.

This time,
touch will not be taken.
It will be offered.
It will be safe.
It will be mine

The Touch Interlude

If you still flinch at a hand raised too quickly, or feel your skin crawl at an unexpected touch, you are not broken. Your body is just remembering. It learned that touch could be a weapon, and it has never forgotten its job to protect you.

Healing this is slow work, and it starts with you. It's okay if the only touch that feels safe right now is your own. You are allowed to take all the time you need to rewrite this language. You have the right to decide who gets to be close to you and when.

Your "no" is sacred, and your "yes"—when you are ready—will be, too. You are relearning safety in your own skin, and that is a quiet, powerful victory.

This Is What Surviving Looks Like

It doesn't look like a movie.
It doesn't look like clean slates
and scripted happy endings.

It looks like waking up with a heavy chest
you swear it's made of stone—
and still dragging yourself out of bed,
still forcing air into tired lungs.

It looks like shaking hands
striking matches, lighting candles,
whispering names of the gone
into silent rooms that will never answer back.

It looks like spills everywhere—
tears in produce,
laughter that feels like it belongs to someone else,
smiles cracked down the middle.
It looks like canceling plans
because your heart is too weary to play pretend.

It looks like writing the story yourself-
in ink no one can steal,
with a voice they tried to silence,
with pages they told you weren't yours to fill.
It looks like reclaiming the pen—
over and over again.

It looks like forgiving yourself
for the mornings you can't be brave,
for the nights you fall asleep still trembling,
for every time you whisper "I can't"
and then keep breathing anyway.

It looks like survival—
but not the shiny kind they glorify.
Not the version tied up in neat bows
and framed in tidy quotes.
No, this survival is jagged.
This survival is bloody-knuckled.
This survival sometimes hates itself.
This survival sometimes begs for rest.

And still—
this survival breathes.
It bleeds.
It shakes.
It holds on when there's nothing to hold.
It is not triumphant every day.
But it is real.

This is what surviving looks like.
It looks like me.
It looks like you.
It looks like the parts they'll never put in films—
and that's exactly why it matters.

We are still here.
Messy.
Hurting.
Healing.
Alive.

And that is no small thing.

This Is What Surviving Looks Like Interlude

Survival isn't meant to look pretty.

If you believe your survival wasn't pretty enough to deserve to be noticed, remember this: it's not **your** audition, and **you** don't need applause for it to count.

Your wounds don't need to be carved into inspiration, and you don't need to sand down the edges of your story so it fits neatly into someone else's idea of strength.

Surviving is enough. It's not tidy or polished. It's the scar that still itches, the breath that still catches, the mornings you rise without knowing why—but you still rise.

Strength isn't always loud or seen. Sometimes it's just existing when your body wants to collapse. Sometimes it's choosing food when your stomach twists or dragging yourself through a day no one will ever see .

That is survival. That is worthy.

You don't owe anyone the edited version of your life, the one with the jagged pieces hidden away. The hardest parts matter. The parts that nearly broke you... they matter .

You belong here in all your unfinishedness, even when you're tired and can't see why.

If you've felt like your survival wasn't beautiful enough to be celebrated, I hope you know it still matters.

You don't have to become someone else's inspiration or package your pain into something uplifting.

**Still healing.
Still trying.
Still alive.**

And that—exactly that—is enough.

"LaCapra Theory holds that there are two fundamental forms of remembering traumatic events: 'acting out' and 'working through'."

Kintsugi Art: Japanese Art

Kintsugi is the ancient art of mending broken pottery with lacquer dusted in gold, silver, or platinum, and it usually looks like it has a little glitter to it as it shimmers.

Its message is clear and uncompromising: what has been broken is not ruined. A vessel repaired with gold becomes more precious, not less—just like us after pain or trauma, we can emerge stronger, more luminous.

This philosophy refuses to disguise damage. Cracks are not hidden; they are gilded, turned into beauty. Every fracture is honored as part of the object's story, proof of survival rather than shame.

We are not pottery, yet the metaphor holds. Our scars are not erasures of who we are but inscriptions of what we've endured. To see them as golden shimmery seams is to reclaim our light.

We rise with our cracks intact, refusing to let trauma dull our shine.

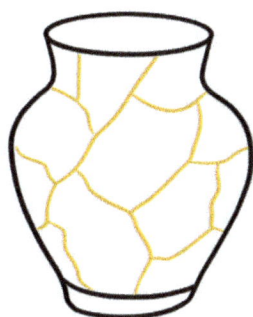

Resources

If you need help or someone to talk to, I always recommend a good therapist. I found one that is amazing at helping me. If you need someone right now, here are some resources:

Suicide and Crisis Lifeline:
988
(you can call or text them)

988lifeline.org

National Sexual Assault Hotline:

1-800-656-4673

They also have a chat option
at rainn.org

About the Author

Kayla Namio is a writer, advocate, and survivor dedicated to breaking the silence around trauma and mental health. She lives with her beloved dogs and bearded dragon, who inspire her to keep choosing hope.

Thank you so much for reading this vulnerable outlet. I wanted to let others know you're not alone. I'm still working on putting my words out there, but I thought this could be my first step in getting the words said.

My family has been so supportive and helpful while I try to figure it all out, and my therapist has been so patient during her time with me.

www.ingramcontent.com/pod-product-compliance
Lightning Source LLC
LaVergne TN
LVHW022011080426
835513LV00009B/668